PR
"The SAVI

MW00583988

"The SAVI Singing Actor offers students and teachers an easy-to-grasp approach to some of the most common challenges singing actors face. In a series of handy exercises, loaded with mnemonic devices that make these techniques easy to understand and apply, author Charles Gilbert dissects and delivers the SAVI techniques in ways that translate quickly to classroom study and performance. Long a leader in Musical Theatre pedagogy, Charles Gilbert has finally delivered an essential text that belongs on every serious teacher's shelf. His ideas and exercises are certain to find their way into your studio, as they have mine."

-Joe Deer
Distinguished Professor of Musical Theatre,
Wright State University
Author, *Acting in Musical Theatre, Directing in Musical Theatre*

"I've known Charlie Gilbert—as a producer, performer and pedagogue, as artist, academician and administrator—for 25 years and his SAVI tools are a perfect bridge to 21st century storytelling in musical theatre."

-Forrest McClendon
Tony Nominee, *The Scottsboro Boys*
Lunt Fontanne Fellow. Barrymore Award Winner

For Allen,
with best wishes always.
Charlie

The

SAVI

Singing Actor

Your Guide to Peak Performance on the Musical Stage

CHARLES GILBERT

Contents

CHAPTER 1

Introduction

Peak Performance

Almost nothing compares to the high you get when you're singing a song onstage and you know you're killing it.

Am I right? I'll bet you and I share a passion for making memorable work on the musical stage.

Chances are you recognize the ecstasy on the face of the dude in the back, the one with no glasses and a bad haircut, playing Nathan Detroit in *Guys and Dolls* in 1970. That's me, spreading my artistic wings back in eleventh grade! For nearly fifty years, the musical theater has been my life's work, and this is where the journey began.

And what an amazing journey it's been! I quickly discovered I had more to contribute as a director, a composer and an educator than a performer. I wrote music and lyrics for a slew of shows, one of which caught Stephen Sondheim's attention and provided the idea for his musical *Assassins*. I got to start the BFA musical theater program at The University of the Arts in Philadelphia and oversee it for nearly 20 years. I got to play Sweeney Todd in the movies years before Johnny Depp did (even if my total screen time in Kevin Smith's *Jersey Girl* was under 20 seconds). I helped found an international organization for people like me who teach musical theater at colleges and universities, which gave me an insider's view of the state of the art in musical theater training worldwide. And I had the chance to work with hundreds of singing actors, young and old, beginners and pros, each one of them looking for ways to make perform better.

Maybe you're a high school student or an adult amateur who's just been cast in a musical and you want to begin building a reliable performance technique. Maybe you're a student in a high school or college musical theater program, looking for a way to stand out in classes, auditions, and shows. Maybe you're an early-career professional who misses the discipline and the routines of your school days, or a working singer-actor always on the lookout for ways to keep your tools sharp, stretch your creative muscles, and stay on point in a competitive, challenging field. Or perhaps you're a teacher, a director, or a coach who works with any of the sort of people I named above. If any of these apply to you, we have a lot to talk about.

Common Ground

There's really no such thing as a "typical" musical theater performer. There are as many types of performers as there are types of musicals: grand and intimate, silly and serious, mainstream and experimental, professional and amateur, bel canto and "can belto."[1] Many roads lead to the musical stage, including acting, dance, classical music, improv, stand-up comedy, pop and rock music, even sports. We musical theater performers are a remarkable, colorful and diverse tribe, one where all sorts of people feel at home, and we express ourselves in many different ways.

Even so, there are some things we have in common as members of this tribe. We know that singing for an audience is a glorious experience, an opportunity to express powerful feelings and ideas in ways that deeply move the listener. Great singers have the ability to enchant us, casting a spell that lifts us up out of our everyday, ordinary experience and transports us to something more rare and exalted. Since the dawn of mankind, humans have gathered together to make music and to experience it, an act that is at once communal and also profoundly personal, a magic that strengthens the connection we feel to one another and to our purest private essence.

Lyricist Yip Harburg said it perfectly when he wrote, "Words make you think thoughts. Music makes you feel a feeling. A song makes you feel a thought."[2] Because songs deliver information in such a powerful way, they can penetrate the mind and the heart, leaving an indelible impression.

This accounts for the incredible power of song and its ability to change the world. The legendary American folk singer and social activist Woody Guthrie knew about the power of song. Woody painted the slogan "This machine kills fascists" on his well-worn guitar, and he used his music to rally his listeners in opposition not only to fascists but also to racists and oppressors of all

[1] Beverly Patton and Mary Saunders Barton deserve credit for that felicitous turn of phrase.
[2] Quoted in Harriet Hyman Alonso, *Yip Harburg: Legendary Lyricist and Human Rights Activist* (Middletown CT, Wesleyan University Press, 2012), 35.

sorts. "If the fight gets hot," Woody liked to say, "the songs get hotter. If the going gets tough, the songs get tougher."[3]

Woody knew what we all know, down deep: that a crying baby can be soothed by a lullaby, a grieving congregation can find comfort in a hymn, and a crowd at a rally can be whipped into a frenzy by a fiery song.

Musicals are stories told in song, and in musicals, songs make stuff happen. There are songs of wooing and songs of persuasion, songs that confront us with the truth, songs that make a joyful noise and lift every heart. Musicals make us believe that you can't stop the beat and that the sun will come out tomorrow, that no one is alone and that when you wish upon a star, your dreams come true.

This is the great work of singing onstage, and if it's to be done well, it needs to be taken seriously. Doing great work is important, not just to succeed and stand out in a crowded, competitive field, but also because songs matter. Performing them well is a glorious experience that makes the world a better place.

But chances are, if you're reading this book, there's something standing between you and the kind of work you yearn to create on the musical stage.

Is Something Stopping You?

- Do you feel lost when working on your own, without a director, teacher, or coach to guide you?
- Does your work feel "hit or miss," haphazard, and unreliable when it comes time to present?
- Do you have the nagging suspicion that your work is "phony," "fake," or, worst of all, "cheesy"?
- Do you feel like good singing and good acting technique are at odds with each another?
- Do you struggle to find the kind of details that will make your work convincing and memorable?

---

[3] "Woody Guthrie's Biography," Woody Guthrie Publications, Inc., 2018, www.woodyguthrie.org/biography/biography4.htm.

- Does the pressure of performance cause you to "go blank" and forget what you prepared?

It's a gut-wrenching feeling when you blow an audition or a performance. Even if you've been lucky enough to experience success as a performer, nearly all artists also experience the "queer, divine dissatisfaction" that choreographer Martha Graham described to Agnes de Mille, the "blessed unrest that keeps us marching and makes us more alive than the others."[4] That's why it's crucial for you to be in top form every time you take the stage. Every time you're in an audition, in rehearsal, or performing onstage, you want to be able to deliver great work and feel the pleasure of having "nailed it."

Excellence in singing-acting is elusive, and the pursuit of it is frustrating, often daunting. Other performers–your classmates, your colleagues, your competition–make it look easy. When you're alone in the practice room, you inevitably wonder, *Am I spending my time on the right things? What do the others know that I don't?* Or even, *Why is my shit so lame?*

You may be hampered by fear, either consciously or unconsciously. You may be held back because you lack certain specific and learnable skills that will enable you to communicate more effectively when you sing. You may know those skills but be held back by ineffective self-management, so that there's always a gap between what you intend to do and what you're actually doing. Regardless of where you are in your journey as a developing singing actor, there's a good chance that you're missing crucial information.

The Guide You Need

Don't despair! In the following pages, I'll be your guide on the journey from "meh" to "wow."

Within these pages, you'll discover secrets understood by an elite group of what I call "savvy" singing actors.

---

[4] Agnes de Mille, *Martha: The Life and Work of Martha Graham* (New York: Random House, 1991).

Would you like to be one, too?

In the chapters ahead, I'll introduce you to the SAVI System, my signature approach to training the singing actor.

- Together, we'll define what "excellence" means in this challenging, competitive art form.
- Having defined your goals, you'll learn to train like an elite athlete: deliberately, thoughtfully, and with passion and persistence.
- We'll work on skills that are indispensable, regardless of song or genre.
- I'll show you new ways to look at a song, expanding and deepening your approach to roles and repertoire.
- You'll find new ways to get feedback and support while you work, as well as reliable tools for self-assessment, insight, and inspiration.

The SAVI System was created to help you in any kind of performance-regardless of whether you're in a Broadway show, an opera, a rock show, a recital, or a concert of any sort: any occasion where you're presenting vocal music in a dramatic context. It will give you a greater ability to plan, organize, and execute what you're going to do while you're onstage. As you work on the exercises and activities presented in the SAVI System, you'll discover tools to manage the process of creating behavior, making optimal choices, and executing those choices with ease and expressiveness.

The SAVI System will identify the four fundamental attributes of effective singing-acting contained in the acronym SAVI, and teach you to recognize whether your onstage behavioral choices are **Specific, Authentic, Varied, and Intense**. What's more, you'll learn exercises and procedures that will enable you to bring **maximum SAVI** to your performance.

You'll learn to think like an athlete, building strength, stamina, range, ease, and coordination. You'll build your **behavior vocabulary**, giving you an expanded range of creative expression.

You'll also learn to think like an artist, taking responsibility for the authorship of your performance, crafting a vivid and original set of behaviors every time you sing.

As you explore, you'll discover a way of thinking and working that wraps under, over and around all of these skills. This is the missing ingredient, the catalyst that will start the artistic chain reaction destined to create an explosive response in the hearts and minds of your audience.

Composer Kurt Weill said, "I believe that the musical theatre is the highest, the most expressive, and the most imaginative form of theatre."[5] I pledged my allegiance to the musical theater flag back in the days when I played "good old reliable Nathan," and the pursuit of that ideal continues to stir my soul many years later. Now I'm eager to share the fruits of my pursuits with you so that you can fulfill your own potential. If you want your work to measure up to Kurt Weill's lofty ideal, you need to Get SAVI!

---

[5] Quoted in David Ewen, *American Songwriters: An W. W. Wilson Biographical Dictionary* (New York: H. W. Wilson, 1987), 430.

CHAPTER 2

Quick-Start Guide

There's a lot of ground to cover in the following chapters, so it's understandable if you're feeling a little daunted by the prospect or impatient to get to what's ahead. Here's a preview of coming attractions, highlights from the coming chapters (not necessarily in the order of the pages that follow). Think of the following as a handy "executive summary," a tablet of 10 commandments, to whet your appetite for what's in store:

10 Axioms for the SAVI Singing Actor

Axiom 1: When you sing onstage, your job is to create behavior that communicates the dramatic event phrase by phrase. (Read more about Axiom 1 in Chapter 3 and more about Behavior in Chapter 7.)

Axiom 2: The behavior you create will be most effective when it is Specific, Authentic, Varied, and Intense—in other words, when it is "SAVI." (Chapter 3 is where we'll get to know these four words intimately.)

Axiom 3: For Maximum SAVI, you must work on the singer as well as the song. Train like an athlete to optimize your ability to create and organize behavior. (Jump to Chapter 5 to learn how you can "train to gain.")

Axiom 4: Learn to use your face, your most powerful organ of expression. (Chapter 8 is the place to read about the face.)

Axiom 5: Mobilize your eyes. They're a "window to your soul" that will reveal your innermost thoughts if you use them effectively. (Also explored in Chapter 8. Point your eyes there to read more.)

Axiom 6: Adjust your behavior at the beginning of each new musical phrase (the "ding"), and avoid distracting mid-phrase adjustments. These adjustments will create contrast, and contrast creates meaning. (Chapters 6 and 14 will teach you why "It don't mean a thing if it ain't got that 'ding!'")

Axiom 7: A song must be understood and presented as a journey, a series of events that occur in sequence. Navigating the "journey of the song" is like following turn-by-turn directions. (Chapters 3, 6, and 14 are great places to read up on the Journey of the Song.)

Axiom 8: Don't rely on generalized mood or atmosphere to put your song across. Make shish kebab, not applesauce! (More about "applesauce" and Mood Sauce in Chapters 3 and 14.)

Axiom 9: Craft your performance carefully, the same way a song is crafted, with clarity and economy. Keep revising and improving your choices until your performance is the best you can make it. Your work needs the appearance of spontaneity, but you won't achieve that by winging it. (Read more about Crafting in Chapter 16.)

Axiom 10: Quality output requires quality input. Sentience is a key to success. (Chapter 11 explains you why it's so important to "come to your senses" and "get ouchable!")

Now What?

There you have it, friends, the accumulated wisdom of nearly fifty years of teaching and musical theater performances, distilled into ten commandments, a minyan of axioms.

In the following chapters, I'll explain and explore each of these statements. I'll provide examples and evidence to back up my claims.

Best of all, I'll share the unique exercises I've created that will help you put those principles into practice.

Bookmark this chapter so you'll come back and read these ten axioms again and again.

Ready? Let's get to it!

CHAPTER 3

The ABCs of SAVI

"Let's Start at the Very Beginning."

The SAVI System of Singing-Acting is built on a handful of fundamental principles. These core concepts are derived from decades of experience, observing singing actors at work, making new work, and studying what teachers, songwriters and creators have said about the nature of song and the craft of performing a song. Later in this chapter, I'll introduce an exercise-the first of many-where you'll get a chance to apply these concepts, but first, we should spend a little time going over the basic premises of the SAVI System.

Axiom 1: The Job of the Singing Actor

When you sing onstage, your job is to create behavior that communicates the dramatic event phrase by phrase.

Axiom 1 of the SAVI System is a declaration of purpose, a single powerful statement that contains three important ideas:

1. The singing actor *creates behavior*.
2. That behavior is chosen for its ability to *communicate the dramatic event*.
3. Finally, those choices are organized *phrase by phrase*, because songs are made of phrases and each phrase

has its own particular role to play in the overall *journey of the song*.

When I say *behavior*, I'm referring to the ways you use your face, your body and your voice to express the drama of the song. *Behavior* includes the movements of your eyes, the expression on your face, your gestures, your movements, your phrasing, your timbre (or vocal color), the quality of your breath, and even the way you shape your vowels and enunciate your consonants. Behavior is what makes Ethel Merman's Mama Rose different from Patti LuPone's, Bette Midler's Dolly different from Carol Channing's, and your performance of any song uniquely yours.

Behavior is the heart of the SAVI System. Whether you're singing in a class, a rehearsal, a performance or the practice room, your job is to create behavior that communicates the dramatic life of the song. Your shrugs, sighs, glances and grimaces are like a painter's brushstrokes or the words in a poem. They give the audience important information about what's going on and how they should feel about it.

If you've been told there's "something missing" in your singing-acting, chances are you're failing to create behavior consistently while you sing. If you already understand what it means to create behavior while you sing, good for you! You can still learn to make a greater variety of choices and organize and execute those choices more optimally.

I recognize that singing a song well is no easy task, but that's only the beginning of your job as a singing actor. Singing well is a good place to start, and great singing is a special sort of thrill, but you know what? Broadway's stages are crowded with performers whose singing is not particularly awesome but who have something else—a presence, a vitality—that comes from knowing how to create behavior onstage while they sing. It's the intangible thing any director or conductor worth working with is counting on you to bring into the room: an ability to create behavior that will bring the drama to life.

To help you understand the importance of Axiom 1 as a crucial first step on the road to successful singing-acting, here are a few additional principles that are so fundamental they're called the ABCs of SAVI Singing-Acting.

ABC = Always Be Creating

Axiom One says, "Your job is to *create* behavior."

Creators are makers, and when you sing, you make something original, a creation that is uniquely yours. Embrace your role as the author of your performance, and you'll be well on your way to new levels of expressiveness and artistic satisfaction.

Every song is a journey, but not the kind where you ride the express train along a familiar route to a beloved destination. No, the art of singing onstage is more like navigating a crowded street on a little motor scooter, like the one I use to travel the streets of Philadelphia. You can't just be a passenger when you take the journey of a song; you've got to take the wheel and navigate its many twists and turns.

Singing well can be difficult, but creating behavior while you sing is even harder. It requires a complicated sort of multitasking that involves a number of different regions of the brain. Successful singing-acting requires focused, coordinated effort both prior to and during the performance. The good news is, your brain is capable of amazingly complex tasks, and if you're like most people, you're only using a fraction of its incredible capacity. Just like an operating system upgrade, the exercises of the SAVI System will expand your capacity for multitasking to help you make the most of what you've got.

ABC = Always Be Choosing

The singing actor creates behavior by making *choices*. What vocal color, facial expression, gesture, inflection or particular detail will you choose to add clarity and impact to each moment in a song? Through an exhaustive process of trial and error, "bit by bit," you will assemble a performance from a series of choices, understanding that, as Sondheim observes in his song "Putting It Together," "every minor detail is a major decision."

With the proper training, you can acquire a wide range of vocal, facial and physical behaviors, an extensive *behavior vocabulary* to choose from at any given moment in a performance. Building up your behavior vocabulary is an important start because, without easy access to a range of options, you're likely to make choices that seem familiar, safe, or obvious as a way of minimizing risk. Even worse, you may make no choices at all. We've all struggled to express ourselves in a sentence, a paragraph or a written essay, and by now you've surely discovered that you can't express grown-up ideas with a child's vocabulary. The same is true for creating expressive behavior when you sing.

When I say the singing actor's job is to "create behavior," I'm not suggesting that just any kooky, random, arbitrary choice that occurs to you on a whim will do. Quite the contrary: you need to delve deep into what acting teacher Uta Hagen calls "the intersection of psychology and behavior."[6] Stanislavski scholar Jean

[6] Uta Hagen, *A Challenge for the Actor* (New York: Scribner, 1991), 50.

Benedetti puts it like this: "Acting is *created* behaviour, prepared spontaneity, something which looks like life but is, in fact, a selection from life, organized in such a way to make an audience participate in the events being shown."[7]

Your job as a singing actor is to create behavior that is appropriate to a specific moment in a particular dramatic event, one that reinforces and reveals the soul of the character and the truth at the heart of the moment.

Making choices requires courage, since you're sticking your neck out every time you choose *this* and not *that*. It requires self-awareness so that you can be sure you're doing what you intend to do. It requires patience and a willingness to iterate, just like a writer or composer keeps revising until they've found the perfect way to express a feeling or idea. Last but not least, making choices requires intelligence so that you can tell which option is the best one when it's time to decide.

ABC = Always Be Communicating

Axiom 1 says it's your job to create "behavior that **communicates** the dramatic event."

A song is a structured form of utterance in which words, phrases and sentences have been organized by means of tempo, pitch, rhythm and pattern into a temporal experience, one that unfolds sequentially in the act of performance. While the words of a song have meaning—in most cases, anyway—it's the song's musical elements that organize the way we experience those words to give them structure, variety, emphasis and, ultimately, clarity and impact.

A song is like a blueprint for performance. It's a set of instructions that, no matter how extensive and elaborate they may seem, remain fundamentally incomplete until you bring them to life. The elements that you contribute to a performance–tone and timbre, facial expression, gesture and body language–can transform a

---

[7] Jean Benedetti, *Stanislavski and the Actor: The Method of Physical Action* (London: Methuen, 1998), 4. I have retained Benedetti's British spellings and emphasis.

song from a blueprint into a soaring cathedral. Your ability to do that, however, will depend on your ability to read that blueprint and take advantage of the clues the songwriter(s) incorporated in the music and text.

The French word for song is *chanson*, and words sung to music become, quite literally, *enchanted*. They are transformed into a powerful spell that has the power to change hearts and minds. Once you routinely and deliberately use singing as a form of *communication*, your songs will change the world.

The words "communication" and "community" have the same root word, "common," from the Latin *communis*, meaning "shared by all or many." One who communicates shares something of him or herself: words, experiences, insights, identity and presence. The act of singing, of communication through song, is fundamentally generous. As a SAVI singing actor, you'll learn to cultivate that spirit of generosity, and to understand that your performance is a gift to be given to an audience.

ABC = Always Be Changing

Songs unfold over time, and the art of singing-acting involves making many choices in succession. **Moments of change**-the moments when you make a transition from one choice to the next-are the most important moments in the life of a song. You must know *when* to change and *what* to change in order to keep the song unfolding as a living, dynamic theatrical experience.

The word "always" in the phrase "Always Be Changing" doesn't mean "constantly," since constant change would result in random, chaotic behavior. It is more precise (but, alas, less catchy) to say, "At the start of each phrase in a song, there is a perfect opportunity to make an adjustment or change, and your new choice should reflect the dramatic event as it is evolving in the *present moment*." That's why Axiom 1 concludes with three words that are a powerful key to SAVI singing acting: **"phrase by phrase."**

Your job is to be constantly creating, choosing behavior that conveys the essence of each moment, and changing that behavior when the song requires it. As you do, you'll craft a varied sequence of specific individual choices to be executed in coordination with the musical event of the song. It's as simple as ABC!

D'ye Savvy SAVI?

It's a happy accident that the acronym "SAVI" sounds like "savvy," a word derived from the Spanish word *saber* and the French *savoir*, both of which mean "to know." Like the French term *savoir faire,* which means "expertise," "savvy" refers to a kind of shrewdness or practical knowledge.

You need not just wisdom but also "street smarts" to guide you on your adventures in singing-acting, and to know SAVI is to be savvy. It's a versatile term: you can use it as an adjective ("your work is very SAVI"), a noun ("Got SAVI?") or even a verb (though it's best to talk like a pirate when asking, "D'ye savvy?"). It's also a mnemonic, created to help you remember the four fundamental attributes of effective singing-acting. Let's meet them now, shall we? Here come the stars of our show:

Specificity! Authenticity! Variety! And... Intensity!

S is for Specificity

The S of SAVI stands for **Specificity**, and the ability to be specific is the first key to successful singing-acting. To be specific is to choose *how* you will communicate as well as *what* you will communicate.

Here are some of the most important ways a singing actor must be specific:

- Being specific to the dramatic event of the song and to each phrase or moment in that event.
- Being specific to the text, the precise meanings of the words and the implications of their syntax, diction and rhetoric.[8]
- Being specific to the music, which means both scrupulous attention to the details of vocal delivery specified in the score and an awareness of the information contained in the accompaniment.
- Being specific in your understanding of the ways in which the present phrase is both similar to and different from its preceding phrases.
- Being specific not only to the meanings and feelings created by the text and the music, but also to the precise moments when changes occur, since these moments present opportunities to make corresponding adjustments in behavior.
- Being specific to the other characters onstage and the environment, which requires an awareness of what's just happened and how the world of the play or musical is changing at any given moment.

An actor's choices must be deeply rooted in the **dramatic event**, the **given circumstances,** and the **present moment.** This requires an incisive understanding of the content and meaning of

---

[8] For starters, this means you must never sing a word whose meaning you don't understand. No, seriously. Take out your phone and Look. It. Up. This is a rookie mistake, and it continues to surprise me how often it happens.

each phrase and an awareness of how it differs from the phrase(s) that came before it.

Making a specific choice implies that you will consider a universe of possibilities and choose the one that seems best suited to your interpretation of a particular moment. This requires specific control over the various forms of behavior you use to express yourself. Is this phrase loud or soft? How loud? How soft? Are certain words to be accented? Are certain words best sung legato or staccato? What kind of timbre or vocal color is to be employed, and on which words? Where is your focus—that is, where are your eyes looking when you sing at this moment? What kind of facial expression are you using? Which muscles of the face are involved in making that expression? What is your stance like? Your body language?

I'm bombarding you with questions to give you an idea of the number of different decisions you must make for each phrase of a song. Considering how you're going to use your face, voice and body to express the feelings and ideas in each and every phrase of your song is exhausting work, but boy, is it important!

Being specific means scrupulously executing the details you've decided on in collaboration with the composer, the lyricist, the director, the choreographer and the conductor. In the parlance of the professional theater, you must routinely "hit your marks." In a show, you're a member of a large group of artists performing complex tasks in close quarters for audiences with high expectations. Under these circumstances, precise attention to detail is mandatory. You will be expected to "nail it" again and again, which requires exceptional concentration, intensity and awareness of detail in rehearsals and performances.

Inside Out and Outside In

It's just as important to be specific about the ***inner life*** of a song-the given circumstances, the psychology of the character, and all the other choices that go into creating subtext-as it is to be specific about the **outer life** of a song–the vocal, facial and physical behavior which is an outward manifestation of that inner life.

Inner and outer life have the power to affect one another. To use a fancy term, they have a **duplex relationship**, a line of communication in which signals can travel simultaneously in opposite directions. When there's a change in subtext or the inner psychological landscape of a song, there should be some sort of corresponding behavioral change; conversely, a change in your exterior behavior has the potential to alter the way you feel and your inner psychological state. Konstantin Stanislavski, the Russian actor, director and teacher who transformed actor training in the twentieth century, used the term **psycho-physical** to describe this interrelationship, and one of the goals of actor training is to cultivate the pathways that connect your physical and psychological energies. Ideally, an adjustment made in one will always produce a corresponding change in the other.

Axiom 1 instructs you to "communicate the dramatic event," and that means you must know who is doing what to whom in your song, and what makes that action important. The singer must determine who is singing, who is being sung to, what the circumstances are, what is being done, and what is at stake.

Making specific choices requires analysis, a forensic investigation of the text of the song and, when applicable, the musical it comes from. In Chapter 12, we'll take a look at Stanislavski's fundamental questions as an essential component of song preparation.

Signs of Insufficient Specificity

If your work is not specific, it will of course appear general, the quality Stanislavski declared to be "the enemy of all art." If your work lacks specificity, every moment will seem similar to every other moment. Instead of creating behavior that communicates the dramatic event, you may be making one of these common mistakes:

- The work of singing and your sincere effort to do a good job may pervade every moment of your performance.
- Your shyness and lack of confidence may be the predominant quality of every moment.
- Conversely, the work of singing-acting and your eager desire to please, charm, or entertain your listener may be apparent in every moment.

Many actors hesitate to make a choice for fear of making the wrong choice. If you face that dilemma, here's a surprising bit of good news: there are many moments in a song when *any* choice will do. Seriously, you will come to realize there are any number of occasions where the simplest of choices–a shift of focus, an adjustment of your stance, an almost insignificant gesture–can be made effective and meaningful in the context of performance.

To know whether your work is sufficiently specific or too general, you need feedback. After all, it's difficult to judge without objective evidence. That's why I'm a proponent of using your phone, camera or laptop to record yourself if you're working alone. Video will make it abundantly clear whether you're being specific or general.

Even if you're working with a coach or teacher (or you're coaching someone yourself), video playback is still a powerful tool. Looking at the evidence together, you can discuss what's working and what's not with calm objectivity. It works for athletes of all sorts, and it'll work for you, too.

It's important to recognize that doing and judging are separate mental processes that can get in the way of each other. When you're living in the moment, give yourself permission to act freely and fully, without self-criticism. After the scene is over, get clear, objective feedback—either in the form of video or the personal comments of a director, teacher or coach—to help you evaluate whether you're making a sufficient number of choices and whether those choices are specific and useful. We'll dig deeper into the notion of Specificity in Chapter 12, exploring procedures for song analysis and other ways to maximize specificity.

A is for Authenticity

"I've been told nobody sings the word 'hunger' the way I do. Or the word 'love,'" wrote Billie Holiday in her memoir, *Lady Sings the Blues*.[9] Lady Day distilled her painful life experiences into unforgettable vocal performances, and you can hear her compellingly authentic style in recordings of songs like "You Don't Know What Love Is" and "Strange Fruit."

The British actor, director, and writer Simon Callow recognized the same quality in the work of legendary singer and actor Paul Robeson, who sang spirituals like "Go Down Moses" and show tunes like "Ol' Man River" with a deep and powerful sense of authenticity: "The astonishing voice that, like the Mississippi in the most famous number in his repertory ["Ol' Man River"], just kept rolling along, seemed to carry within it an inherent sense of *truth*. There was no artifice; there were no vocal tricks; nothing came between the listener and the song. It commanded effortless attention; perfectly focused, it came from a very deep place, not just in the larynx, but in the experience of what it is to be human."[10]

Authenticity is expected of any actor in the modern era: you've got to "bring the realness" to your work. Truthful expression makes it possible for your audience to relate to you as a real person, and to understand and empathize with what you're singing about. Finding a way to create and express yourself truthfully within the artificial conventions of song and dance is a challenge every singing actor must face.

Nowadays, much of the acting we see is on screens, where the camera can zoom in for the most intimate of close-ups. This has come to influence our notion of what seems "real" and "authentic."

[9] Billie Holiday and William Dufty, *Lady Sings the Blues: 50th Anniversary Edition* (New York: Harlem Moon, 2006), 195.
[10] Simon Callow, "The Emperor Robeson," *New York Review of Books*, February 8, 2018, www.nybooks.com/articles/2018/02/08/emperor-paul-robeson/.

Stage performers, however, must be able to create behavior that projects to the back row of a large auditorium. When you're in a show, the director will exhort you, like Mama Rose in *Gypsy*, to "Sing out, Louise!" and "Smile, baby!" You'll be told to "cheat out," to face the audience rather than your scene partner onstage.

Of course, all of this seems fundamentally at odds with being truthful onstage. What's more, there is no behavior in real life that resembles singing-acting. Singing on the stage is inherently an artificial act; we don't do it in real life, so there's no way it can ever seem entirely lifelike. Director Tadashi Suzuki attempts to address this paradox in his book *The Way of Acting*: "The art of stage performance cannot be judged by how closely the actors can imitate or recreate ordinary, everyday life on the stage. An actor uses his words and gestures to try to convince his audience of something profoundly true. It is this attempt that should be judged."[11]

If you find this all confusing, don't worry. You'll get a lot of contradictory instructions in the course of your musical theater career, and finding ways to reconcile those contradictions is a big part of your job as a singing actor. Musical theater performance involves a number of highly technical component skills, including voice, music, dance and speech. Meanwhile, you may hear your acting teachers encouraging you to "be yourself," to draw upon your own experiences to achieve a sense of personal truth. How do you find the right balance between being too "stagey" and too casual?

Acting teachers who employ the pedagogy of Sanford Meisner can be very persuasive when they tell their students, "Leave yourself alone!" As a result, I've encountered many young actors who seem to think that doing *nothing* will eliminate everything "unnatural" from their performance. Instead, your goal should be to create only as much behavior as you need to communicate the dramatic event, and then rehearse those choices until your practiced ease makes them seem natural.

---

[11] Tadashi Suzuki, *The Way of Acting: The Theatre Writings of Tadashi Suzuki,* translated by J. Thomas Rimer (New York: Theatre Communications Group, 1986), 5.

It takes time and skill to achieve authenticity in singing-acting. Many complex tasks, which at first seem mechanical and artificial, become habitual and seem natural in time, and it's no different with singing-acting. Think about how walking was mechanical and unnatural when you took your first steps as a toddler. You took plenty of falls at first, but with practice, you got the hang of it.

In our post-modern era, it's common to see musicals that mix elements of vaudeville, diegetic song[12], and Brechtian commentary along with complex characters and compelling situations. Audiences want to believe that the character they see onstage is an authentic human being, living truthfully under imaginary circumstances, but they also respond enthusiastically to virtuosic performances and outsize "larger than life" personalities. You've got to bring the realness, but you can't leave out the awesomeness. What an incredible, exciting challenge!

Cue the "Magic If"

As a singing actor, you must find a way to bring your authentic self to the fictional given circumstances of the song or play. Stanislavski recognized this as a core skill for any actor, and developed an approach to it he called the "Magic If." As an actor, you must be able to behave "as if" any circumstance or set of circumstances were true. This requires a specific understanding of the circumstances of a scene (or song), and also the ability to imagine that those circumstances are really affecting you.

The practice room is the ideal environment in which to explore the "Magic If." Construct an imaginary circumstance (defining who, what, where, and why) for yourself, and then see what happens when you sing a song under those imaginary circumstances, such as:

- an accused person pleads with a jury
- a lover woos his beloved

---

[12] The term "diegetic music" refers to music that is part of the fictional situation. A diegetic song is one in which the act of singing the song is part of the dramatic event, for example, when Sally Bowles sings the title song of the musical *Cabaret*.

- a timid employee challenges a brutal, intimidating boss
- a parent threatens a rebellious child
- a rebellious child confronts a strict parent

For training purposes, it doesn't matter whether the circumstances fit the song; indeed, there's much to be learned from stretching your imagination and exploring the wide diversity of possible behaviors that emerge from both appropriate and provocatively inappropriate circumstances.

Improvisation is an invaluable tool in the acting studio, giving students a chance to "playfully" experience what it's like to live under imaginary circumstances. Many of the SAVI exercises in this book incorporate elements of dramatic improvisation and fantasy to liberate your imagination and strengthen your ability to sing truthfully under a wide range of circumstances.

Warning Signs of Inauthenticity

Though truthful performance can take an infinite variety of forms, there are a few common behavioral phenomena that occur while singing that inevitably scream, "Fake!" Many of us can't help doing them when we sing. We may not even be aware that we're doing them, but by making these choices, we send a signal to the spectator that our behavior is inauthentic, not lifelike. By becoming aware of these behavioral phenomena and addressing them at the technical level, it's possible to make considerable, rapid progress toward greater authenticity in stage expression. Here are three prime offenders:

- a rigid, fixed gaze
- a blank, distorted or frozen face
- a tense, braced-up body

If you're singing in a recording studio, these don't matter, of course. Performing in front of an audience, however, requires you to overcome these challenges. Even recitalists and choral singers need to remain alive and expressive while they sing.

The exercises and procedures you'll read about in the coming chapters will help you address each of these, in turn restoring a more natural and expressive use of the eyes, face and body when you sing. You'll learn to "get ouch-able" so that you can initiate behavior impulsively at the onset of a phrase. You'll learn to "mobilize your eyes" and develop a "thinking eye." You'll find ways to bring greater vitality, variety and truthfulness to your facial expressions, and discover that you "play your ace when you use your face." With patient and purposeful practice on your own or in a group, you'll condition yourself so that, when the time comes in rehearsal or performance, you'll be prepared to express yourself with greater authenticity.

V is for Variety

The V of SAVI stands for **Variety**, the so-called "spice of life" and an essential ingredient of all successful singing-acting. The variety show is one of the ancestors of the modern musical, and to this day, variety in an important consideration in the construction of most musicals. In the late nineteenth century, variety shows like vaudeville, burlesque and revue enjoyed great popularity with audiences, who experienced a performance as a banquet offering multiple "courses" of sensory pleasures: a pretty girl followed by a beautiful singer, followed in turn by a magician or a comedian or a talking dog.

To sing with variety, you need to recognize that each phrase offers you a unique set of opportunities to create behavior. The best singing-acting gives listeners the impression that each new phrase or moment is somehow distinct from previous moments.

Things that are alive are always in a state of change, and the reverse is true as well: things that do not change don't seem lifelike. Drama is by its very nature dynamic, not static; it depicts characters propelled by forces of change to moments of crisis and, ultimately, moments of climax. Effective stage behavior must have variety if it is to successfully project that dynamic quality and reflect the changes taking place as the dramatic event unfolds.

Variety creates contrast, and contrast creates meaning; that's the natural law at the heart of Axiom 6. When spectators detect a change onstage, there's a part of their brain that begins to puzzle over its significance: *What just happened? He was looking there, but now he's looking here! She was singing softly, but then she suddenly got loud! What's it all mean?* Our brains are hardwired to seek that information, and if we don't get it–if there's no change, no new information detected by our senses–we as an audience become disengaged from an experience very quickly. How quickly? In my experience, if you haven't made any sort of change in twenty or thirty seconds, your listener is already becoming less fully engaged.

Variety is a way of beguiling the audience by mingling the familiar and the surprising, knowing that introducing something fresh and unexpected is a surefire way to grab an audience's attention when it starts to wander. By crafting your performance using the same fundamental principle that is used in the construction of a musical, your work is guaranteed to become more engaging and more meaningful.

Applesauce and Shish Kebab

Ready for a snack break? Take a look at these two pictures of food and tell me what's different between them.

The first is a dish of applesauce, the second a Middle Eastern dish of skewered meats and vegetables called shish kebab.

Applesauce is delicious, of course, but with just one ingredient, every sweet and smooth spoonful tastes just like every other spoonful.

Shish kebab is a different sort of dish. One look tells you that it's made up of a bunch of different bits, and the skewer serves an important function in organizing them all into a unit.

Your job is to create performances that are like shish kebab, not applesauce. An "applesauce" performance is general and mood-driven, while a "shish kebab" performance is carefully conceived to highlight the specific content of each individual phrase.

"Applesauce" performances aren't always sweet. I've seen eager applesauce, angsty applesauce, angry applesauce, sexy applesauce; there's all sorts of ways to generalize. If every bite tastes the same—if the phrases aren't differentiated—then there's a fundamental flaw in your singing-acting technique. What you're striving to achieve is not a smooth flow in your performance, but something that is appealing in its variety of textures and flavors.

Reasons for a Lack of Variety

Making a clear and specific choice for each phrase of a song is the best way to maximize variety in your performance. If it's that simple, why doesn't it happen routinely? Maybe you haven't paid enough attention to the clues in the text and the music or fully understood the dramatic circumstances. By being diligent and thoughtful in your pursuit of opportunities to create variety, you'll discover what is distinct and different about each moment and what makes it different from its predecessor.

Do you get distracted by the technical challenges of musical execution and vocal production? Singing can consume so much of your awareness that you're left with no attention to devote to the dramatic event. If a passage is especially complex vocally or musically, you may find yourself unable to pay attention to the ways in which a new moment might be different than its predecessor.

When you learn a piece of new material, you practice it until it becomes familiar, like a habit, so that you can execute it with greater ease and less conscious attention. However, routine can be a curse as well as a blessing. If you get into the habit of "going with the flow" in a well-rehearsed performance, you'll miss out on the opportunities that bring it to life. It is the onset of new thoughts and events, the occurrences that disrupt the flow of the drama, that bring the performance to life, and result in work that is varied and truthful.

Fear is another factor that may be limiting your capacity for variety. We all have an understandable tendency to stick with what is known; if we hit upon a choice that feels right in a particular moment, we want to keep doing it, since our expectation is that it will continue to be right. As musicians and vocalists who are scrupulously attentive to the myriad details and technical challenges that a score presents, we know there are countless ways to get something wrong, and inevitably we tense up slightly, bracing ourselves for the mistake that is lurking just around the corner. But as we brace up in anticipation of a mistake, we diminish our ability to recognize the possibilities for creating new life in the coming moment.

What's more, many songs have a kind of uniformity or consistency in their musical and verbal expression that can mislead you as a performer. This is true regardless of genre or when a song was written, though a statistical analysis of half a million songs from the past 50 years finds that pop songs have grown more homogenous in their timbre and pitch transitions.[13] There are songs of all sorts whose singular atmosphere seems to put us in a kind of trance. As we fall under the spell of the song, we resort to generalized behavioral choices and rely excessively on a single focus, facial expression or physical life.

Any song is more interesting when it is performed with attention to behavioral variety. Your song is enhanced, not marred, when you find opportunities to break the spell and "disrupt" the overall mood of the song with changes in focus or behavioral

---

[13] Honest, this isn't a tiresome geezer rant. See Joan Serrà et al., "Measuring the Evolution of Western Contemporary Popular Music." Nature.com. https://www.nature.com/articles/srep00521 (accessed 5/10/2019)

expression. These disruptions will provide highlights and shadows, contours of expression from which a spectator will derive greater meaning. Let the audience be enchanted by the song, but learn to stay fully present and alert to the opportunities to avoid "going with the flow."

One of the things that makes certain songs "theatrical" is the way that variety is integrated into the musical composition itself. You'll see musical notation like the caesura ("railroad tracks") and fermata used to disrupt the temporal flow of these songs. In addition, wordy, rhythmic phrases might be contrasted with others that are simple and sustained, and accompaniments will change texture, key and register abruptly. These musical "quirks" are the stock-in-trade of the theatrical composer, making their songs dramatically effective but too eccentric to be successful away from the stage. (Examples abound, but the work of Mr. Sondheim serves as Exhibit A.)

As a performer in training, you'll want to continually expand your capacity for creating variety. Think about behavior as a closet full of different outfits you can put on or take off when you choose. If your "behavior closet" is bare, stocked with only a few simple or overworn choices, you've got your work cut out for you. Many of the activities and exercises described later in these pages are designed to give you a greater array of choices and to help you feel more comfortable switching from one choice to another.

I is for Intensity

Humans love extremes. Extreme sports, extreme challenges, extreme accomplishments.

Musical theater is full of examples of people going to extremes: of characters pushed to the limit, pushed to either a breakdown or a breakthrough, and of performers pushing the limits of what is possible, challenging the boundaries of skill and endurance in displays of virtuosity. **Intensity** is the quality of heightened emotionality in a singing actor's behavior. Many memorable moments in the musical theater repertoire depict passionate characters reacting to significant events with strong emotion. Music and lyrics serve to intensify emotion on the musical stage, and the successful singing actor must be able to rise to those emotional heights without sacrificing believability or specificity.

All of the arts are capable of delivering an intense experience, a heightened distillation of feeling and insight that leaves the spectator moved and exhilarated. We as an audience crave the intensity of a performance just as we crave it in our intimate relationships. It's no coincidence that the word "climax" shows up in both dramaturgy and sex.

The SAVI singing actor is able to create intensity by bringing *more* when more is needed: more volume, more behavior, more range, more detail, more "wow." Conveying intensity means being comfortable with going to extremes without unnecessary tension. The capacity to create *more*-to sing louder, to sing higher, to be more furious or more tender, to reach farther, move faster, leap higher-is part of the Olympic challenge of singing acting, and you must train for it like an Olympian.

Intense? Or Just Tense?

Students and professionals alike tend to confuse intensity with tension. For instance, in the pursuit of a high level of vocal intensity, a singer may create a great deal of tension in the vocal mechanism. In fact, tension is the opposite of intensity. By way of analogy, think about a car. Intensity is the force of the engine, while tension is what you experience when you apply the brakes, the result of two forces in conflict. Many performers unconsciously associate the sensations of tension with the experience of intensity, but if you take the brakes off, you'll strain a lot less and achieve a better result.

Sometimes excessive tension is a problem of awareness or intention on the part of the singer, but sometimes it's the inevitable consequence of the neurological effects of extreme behavior. When we go to extremes as a performer–singing very loudly or in a high register–that physical act also triggers intuitive responses in the nervous system. These cries awaken the "fight or flight" response in our primitive "lizard brain," causing additional adrenaline to flow, muscles to tense up and sensory awareness to diminish.

Let's face it, all screamers and adrenaline junkies face inevitable burnout. Our bodies, our voices and our souls have a finite capacity for intensity, and we can exhaust that capacity surprisingly quickly.

Actors tend to be vivid and loud because they have a natural affinity for intensity of expression. That's not to say that you have to be loud and flamboyant offstage in order to succeed onstage, but it is unarguable that the capacity for extreme expression is essential to the performer, and an affinity for extremes of expression sure doesn't hurt, either.

Intensity doesn't just mean "be loud," of course. Being able to create intensity onstage is the ability to create *more*, but "more" doesn't always equate to "loud." *More* can mean more subtle, more delicate, more tender. An actor needs to have *more* facial mobility so that his face can be more expressive even when silent. *More* can refer to a more dynamic use of breath, more ease in movement, more lightness and buoyancy. Any sort of *more* is a form of intensity, and the singing actor needs to be comfortable with all of them.

Thus, the "I" of Intensity also implies dynamic range, the ability to consciously vary how much of a certain ingredient or behavior you choose to bring to a particular moment in a performance. The experience of intensity is based on contrast: it's difficult to create the experience of loudness as a musical effect if you play everything loud. It's not enough to build your strength and stamina to be a screamer instead of a singer; you need the ability to sing expressively at every dynamic, at every level of intensity.

Common Intensity Problems

There are several common problems I see students have when it comes to intensity. The first of these is weakness. Lack of intensity is often a lack of strength, either physically (weak muscles and/or vocal cords) or psychologically (a weak will). Of course, the way you get stronger is through exercise, and many of the exercises and études in this book were designed to make you physically and mentally stronger.

As with variety, intensity can be negatively impacted by fear. Sometimes we don't go "all out" with our performances because we're afraid: afraid that something will go wrong, that we'll make a mistake, that we'll seem ridiculous. Patient, persistent work in a supportive environment where your successes are recognized and praised will help you conquer your fears and bring more of what you've got to your performance.

Laziness is another psychological concern facing our intensity as singing actors. Legendary diva Patti LuPone writes, "It's hard, eight shows a week, it's extremely hard. But that's Broadway and it takes muscle to perform on Broadway, eight shows a week…. As they say, 'Broadway ain't for sissies.'"[14] Achieving intensity means being willing to do the work, to train hard and bring your "A game" every single day.

Excessive physical tension can limit your range of motion or range of expression. It's often an unwanted side effect of trying too hard. Deliberate, purposeful practice can help you reduce habitual tension and extend your range as you acquire the habit of bringing more *ease* to your performance. It may seem counter-intuitive, but by allowing yourself to relax into your performance, you will be able to achieve greater intensity.

Finally, a lack of dynamic variation can spoil one's intensity. Intensity sometimes calls for immensity, but beware of becoming addicted to extremes like loud/soft, smooth/staccato. You must be able to provide "more" when it's called for, but don't be that

---

[14] Patti LuPone, "Ramblings from the Road," *Patti LuPone*, www.pattilupone.net/ramblings65.html.

person who "turns it up to eleven" all the time. Listeners get tired and tune that out.

The "Dramatic Event"

The singing actor is a singer who *acts*, and the ability to undertake an action rather than express a feeling is central to the skill set you need to succeed. A bias toward action supports all four of the essential qualities in the SAVI acronym. Your *Specific* answer to the question, "What are you doing now?" is the most important choice you can make. Focusing on action rather than emotion also supports *Authenticity*, since truthful acting is rooted in the reality of doing. Modifying and modulating your action choices from phrase to phrase is a key strategy for achieving *Variety*. Finally, *Intensity* is supported by having a clear sense of the dramatic event, not only of what you are doing in that moment but also of what makes it important.

Axiom 1 acknowledges the **dramatic event** as a key organizing principle in the creative process of the singing actor. A dramatic event presents us with a set of circumstances, either real or imagined, in which a character wants to make something happen. When we frame a song as a dramatic event, when we view it through this lens, it immediately becomes clear that dramatic action is the dynamo that propels the song forward.

Stanislavski refers to the text of a play or song as "verbal action," by which he means that the language you use is active and deployed to make something happen. The amount of effort you use in the course of the phrase corresponds to the action you are undertaking. In other words, within the imaginary "given circumstances" of the world of this song, what do you need to accomplish? How much effort will such an accomplishment take?

Sometimes, in the parlance of the acting studio, we speak of "playing an action," and often acting is playful (with a childlike sense of "make believe"), but when we play an action, we play in earnest. We play to win.

To act, to take action, is to do something, to try to make something happen. Acting Is Doing. A singing actor plays an action. Simple as that.

Let's take a break from theorizing and put these ideas into practice. The SAVI Étude that follows is the perfect way to explore the concepts of Specificity, Authenticity, Variety and Intensity in action.

EXERCISE: Here I Am

In the SAVI System, it's axiomatic that you create your best performance when you work **phrase by phrase**, that is, by giving your full attention to one phrase at a time. "Here I Am," an exercise that consists of a single phrase of music repeated many times, is a way to practice taking advantage of the choice-making opportunities that are found in each individual phrase.

"Here I Am" can be a powerful experience when sung with others in a group, but let's consider it first as a solo exercise.

Here I Am

Charles Gilbert

The melody for "Here I Am" consists of three pitches arranged in a two-measure phrase. It's intentionally rudimentary to remind you to pay attention to the basics, the fundamental building blocks of singing-acting. It's not as effective to do this exercise a cappella, because the pulsing triplets of the accompaniment provide an important foundation of tempo and continuity to support the melody. (There is a karaoke-style accompaniment track available for download on the SAVI Singing Actor site, which is a good resource to have on hand if you want to work on this without an accompanist. See the Appendix for details.)

When you work on the exercise "Here I Am," your first priority should be to become and to remain fully **sentient**, capable of thought and feeling and able to respond to and express those thoughts and feelings while you sing. Sentience starts with acknowledging your environment, the actual place in which you are practicing.

Look around. Take in the appearance of the room and the objects in it, and allow yourself to be aware of how you feel in that room. Use your other senses as well: be aware of the sounds you hear in the background and the smells in the air. Reach out and touch the objects around you as well; feel your face, rub your hands together and stroke the fabric of your clothing to awaken your sense of touch. Come to your senses!

It's also important to take into account how you're feeling when you do this exercise. Are you feeling pressed for time? Tired? Hungry? Annoyed because you just had a quarrel with someone? Scared about singing? Relaxed and well-rested? Open your thoughts to how your day has been so far and the way events in your day have made you feel. Give yourself permission to acknowledge your actual feelings and to express them in your voice and behavior as you work on the exercise.

As the music for "Here I Am" begins to play, don't feel pressured to sing right away. Instead, breathe in and out in time to the music, inhaling quickly at the moment you would breathe if you were beginning to sing and exhaling steadily during the time you'd be singing. Use the first few repetitions of the accompaniment to *think* the words "Here I am" in your inner monologue. Say to yourself, "Here I am, right here, in this particular room at this particular moment, feeling these feelings I am feeling right now." Your goal is to bring your authentic self to the moment. With each repetition of the two-measure musical phrase, take a breath, reawaken your senses and shift your gaze so your eyes fall on something else in the room as you begin the next moment.

When you feel ready, begin to sing the phrase "Here I am," maintaining that quality of sentience, authenticity and connection to the present moment. Pay attention to how each phrase has *a beginning, a middle* and *an end*. Notice how each of these three aspects has its own unique properties:

- Each phrase *begins* with a thought, an impulse to express something, and that impulse leads to an almost instantaneous intake of breath in preparation for **phonation**, or vocal sound. Be conscious of breathing "all at once," quickly and efficiently, in a way that fully prepares you to express that impulse.
- While you are singing, you are in the *middle* of the phrase. Physics teaches us that it takes a lot of energy to launch something, but once it's in motion, inertia and momentum help to keep it going. It took an initial impulse to animate you, but now you're in flight, like an arrow that flies from a bowstring on its way to the target, and you need a different kind of energy to keep the phrase alive.
- The phrase *ends* on the final note, which is often held out. The energy that propelled you as you traveled through the phrase is used up, and you've reached your destination. Allow yourself to release whatever physical effort was required to maintain the phrase and assess whether you have reached your desired target. You're done with output for the moment, and you need some input. When you sing "Here I am" again, that statement must be informed by the awareness that "here" may not be the same place you were previously.

Having sung the phrase once, let yourself be silent during its next musical repetition, but continue to think "Here I am" as you go back to noticing your inner and outer environment. (If you're in a group, notice the others with you, too.) Alternate a phrase of singing and a phrase of silent inner monologue. Bring your conscious awareness to the rhythm of input and output that is a part of this exercise: taking in information from your environment; allowing yourself to notice the quality of your thoughts and the intake of breath; then sending out sound and expression into that environment.

- As you go through this process again and again, you are moving though a cycle of Action, Assessment and Adjustment–the **AAA Cycle,** for short-that is the heart of singing and living truthfully in each moment.

When you start to sing, you begin with an impulse, an *Adjustment*, that propels you from inaction to take your first *Action*. As you reach the end of the phrase, your attention shifts to your partner's response in order to *Assess* the success of your action. (If you are practicing alone, this is an imaginary partner whose response you'll need to invent.) Did you get the response you wanted? Based on your Assessment, you'll make a new *Adjustment*, a choice about the next Action you want to take. Assessment will help you decide what's next. Do I intensify, back off, or try a different tactic?

The three phases of the AAA Cycle correspond to the beginning (Adjustment), middle (Action), and end (Assessment) of your phrase. Pay attention to how each phrase begins with an adjustment, a choice, a decision you make at the beginning of the exercise that moves you from silence to song, and impels you to sing again when it's time to repeat the phrase.

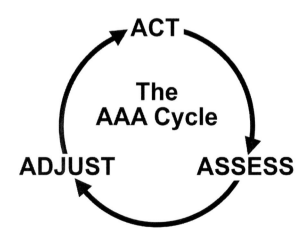

When you're ready, take the pauses out and sing "Here I am" on each repetition of the musical phrase. Though you now have a much shorter period of time between the end of one phrase and the beginning of the next, continue to focus your attention on that moment as a moment of change when it arrives.

After you've gone through a few cycles, you're ready to kick things up a notch and Modulate! When you're working with a live accompanist, you can repeat the first three measures as many times as you want before you start to modulate. (When you're working with a recorded track, the number of repetitions will be predetermined, of course.) As the exercise continues into the fourth measure, you'll be singing in a higher key, which requires a different kind of effort and produces different sensations. Does singing higher change how you feel? Does it lead you to make different sorts of behavior choices? Does it affect your ability to remain sentient?

In the seventh measure, the exercise will modulate to an even higher key. As you ascend to this third level of intensity, you may start to focus more exclusively on your singing and to neglect sentience and behavior. If you find this to be the case, try to focus your awareness on reincorporating those elements that you were neglecting. Remain as sentient and as connected to the AAA Cycle as you are able through the final notes of the exercise.

"Here I Am" with Imaginary Circumstances

To make this exercise a deeper acting experience, invent an imaginary circumstance for yourself. This might be the story arc of a character you're rehearsing, a dramatic situation from a favorite play or musical, or a circumstance you develop on your own. Use the following fundamental questions to delineate the particulars of that circumstance:

- Who am I?
- Where am I?
- What am I doing?
- Why is it important?

- How is this moment different from the preceding moment?[15]

This is an effective way to to practice living truthfully under imaginary circumstances while remaining sentient and active–the work I described in the preceding section. Effective singing-acting requires this sort of multitasking every time you sing, and "Here I Am" helps you strengthen those skills by practicing them apart from the musical and vocal demands associated with a specific piece of musical theater repertoire.

Think of "Here I Am" not a song to be performed but as an exercise, like push-ups or planks. It compels you to be truthful and natural while inhabiting a musical structure and making specific choices at the onset of each new phrase. In the next chapter, I'll introduce some new tools that you can use to make this exercise more Specific, Authentic, Varied and Intense.

Summary

Congratulations! You've reached the end of the longest chapter of the book. I've packed a lot of information into this chapter. What have you learned?

- Your job as a singing actor is to create behavior that communicates the dramatic event phrase by phrase. (That's Axiom 1.)
- As a singing actor, you're always Creating, Choosing, Communicating and Changing. Remember your ABCs!
- Effective singing acting is Specific, Authentic, Varied and Intense. In other words, it's SAVI! D'ye savvy?
- There's a duplex relationship between what you feel and think and the behavior you create to express those thoughts and feelings. It's a two-way street, Inside-Out and Outside-In.

---

[15] More on Fundamental Questions in Chapter 13, when we discuss maximizing Specificity.

- Great singing acting is shish kebab, not applesauce. Every phrase is its own unique opportunity to create behavior.
- "Here I Am" is a great exercise not just for exploring these fundamental concepts but for putting them into daily practice.

CHAPTER 4

Work on the Singer

Over the next eight chapters, we'll explore the essential aspects of musical theater performance technique that apply to any piece in your repertoire, regardless of style or era. My experience coaching hundreds of students through thousands of musical theater songs has helped me identify the most important technical skills you need to succeed as a singing actor. With this in mind, I've created exercises and études like "Here I Am" that will enable you to build your understanding and your mastery of those skills.

It's efficient and effective to work on your singing-acting in a class or group setting. You learn faster when you work with a variety of partners and can "check out" one another's work. Many of the following exercises have a strong element of imitation, leading and following, rather like a ballet class or an exercise class. While the exercises may seem novel at first, they are not meant to be "one-and-done" curiosities; rather, they must be done repeatedly if you want to experience their full value.

Group class, however, is not the only environment where you can undertake the work presented in these chapters. The SAVI exercises and activities can be done alone in the practice room, with a mirror or video camera for feedback. Because so much of the work of a performance has to do with communication, though, you may find it beneficial to explore some of this work with a "practice-room buddy." Working in pairs, you and a peer can support each other as scene partners, serve as one another's "vis-à-vis," provide useful disruption and provocation when required, and offer feedback when desired. Some of these exercises are well suited for one-on-one instruction, and can be introduced in private lessons by a teacher or coach. Ideally, you should try to experience SAVI all three ways: through a mixture of group classes, private tutorials, and solitary practice.

"Work on the Singer as well as the Song"

Proto-pedagogue Stanislavski didn't begin his professional life with a plan to develop a system of actor training. As a young man, he was a performer who studied music, singing and acting in plays and musical theater; in other words, he was not that different from many undergraduate musical theater majors today. As he began to direct productions, including new and realistic works by contemporary authors like Anton Chekhov, he found that the skills that he and his fellow actors possessed weren't sufficient for the challenge of creating believable life onstage.

Though nowadays we speak of the "Stanislavski System," its creator never used that term. In fact, the origins of his system weren't especially systematic. Professor Jean Benedetti, a leading authority on Stanislavski, observes that "[c]ircumstances did not allow Stanislavski to develop his methods other than during rehearsals, in a rather *ad hoc* manner, for some years. None the less the need for a coherent, systematic approach to work, on a daily basis, became more and more apparent, particularly when training young actors."[16] Stanislavski had the advantage of long rehearsal periods and willing participants, but he discovered it was possible to get better, quicker results with actors who were appropriately trained.

As he strove to develop an approach to actor training, Stanislavski identified "work on the self" and "work on the role" as two separate but related endeavors. Building on that profoundly powerful insight, Stanislavski envisioned an approach to acting technique that started by identifying its fundamental "elements."

[16] Jean Benedetti, *Stanislavski: An Introduction*, revised and updated (New York: Routledge, 2004), 53.

He used insights from the then-emergent field of psychology, along with his own practical, personal experiences as an actor, to define the skills that were needed. He then devised a set of procedures that could be used to cultivate those skills outside of rehearsal; indeed, the invention of these procedures was his life's most enduring work. His approach prepared the actor for the true work of rehearsal, which ought to be readying the work for performance rather than training the performers.

Dancers and musicians, as a rule, are more familiar with the simultaneous pursuit of technique work and repertoire work on parallel tracks. Athletes also understand that drills must be done at practice to cultivate skills that will be needed on game day. Stretches at the ballet barre, the scales played by the instrumentalist, and the hours spent on the practice field are not an end unto themselves but a way of developing coordination, strength, flexibility, range, understanding, and, finally, mastery, so that the skills become ingrained as habits and can be accessed without conscious thought during the extreme demands of performance.

Axiom 3 of the SAVI System is my way of stating this fundamental insight from Stanislavski in the language of the singing actor: you must **"work on the singer as well as the song."** Work on the *song* is driven by the demands of the repertoire; that's the type of work you're probably most familiar with. You're used to spending your time in class and in the practice room rehearsing and mastering a bulging binder of songs so that you and your work look as good as possible.

There's a great deal of work on the *singer*, however, that can be undertaken both in class and in the privacy of the practice room that will dramatically prepare you to undertake the challenges of the song. Setting aside the technical demands of a piece sets you free to pay attention to your own developmental needs instead of being a servant to the song. Since working on the singer in class can be done effectively in a group setting, it also has the benefit of greater efficiency, unlike repertoire study, which requires extensive one-on-one studio time.

This book is organized so that the next eight chapters are devoted to "work on the singer," focusing on activities that will improve your skills as a singing actor independent of work on any particular piece. The final five chapters before the conclusion address "work on the song," showing you how to apply the theories I've outlined in this chapter—as well as the technical skills introduced in the previous section—to specific examples of music theater repertoire.

Special Challenges Facing the Singing Actor

The SAVI System's concept of working on yourself as a singer first helps to combat some of the unique and yet all-too-common challenges that singing actors face. The technical issues that occur when music and singing are part of the fundamental expressive vocabulary of a dramatic work include:

Multi-tasking. Musical theater requires its performers to do several things at once, activities that involve separate parts of the brain and body. Thoughts and feelings, sequence and spontaneity, music and language: many aspects of musical theater performance engage multiple regions of the brain simultaneously, often in ways that cause complications or interference.

For instance, the experience of emotion is accompanied by an increase of activity in the ***limbic system***, the part of your central nervous system sometimes referred to as the "lizard brain." The limbic system is in charge of fight, flight, fear, feeding and fornication–the five most basic human drives. Making and executing plans involves a different part of the brain, the ***frontal cortex***, where your so-called "executive function" resides. ***Executive function*** is what you use when you're making conscious choices and carrying out a plan, but when strong emotions are present (including the powerful feelings that arise from the physical act of singing), the lizard brain grabs the wheel and executive function can wind up in the back seat.

Put simply, the part of your brain that *feels* is different from the part of your brain that *plans*, and sometimes it's hard for those two parts to work together. The challenge facing every singing actor is the need to coordinate the "feeling" part and the "planning" part. Cross-training your brain is therefore one of the most important benefits of training with the SAVI System. Many of the SAVI Card exercises and activities are designed to balance and coordinate the relationship between emotion and executive function.

Musical alteration of time. Sometimes a song requires you to develop or sustain a single action, thought, phrase or word in a way that seems "unnatural"—that is, that is sustained for longer than it would be if music were not present in the scene. Music can also speed up or fragment the flow of time and action, and the singing actor is frequently called upon to change behavior in coordination with musical timing. Many SAVI exercises focus on the challenge of what choreographer Agnes de Mille referred to as "acting in tempo."

Acting with an imaginary partner. The musical theater repertoire often calls for you to act while alone onstage, sometimes pretending to interact with a specific character, while other times you are interacting with the audience or appearing to think out loud. These soliloquy moments are some of the most important and memorable moments in the literature, and they require a particular set of technical skills that you can practice even when you're alone.

Working with the audience as a partner. Singers work more actively with an audience than actors in a play do, even in "realistic" musicals where the audience is behind the so-called "fourth wall." In a song or a musical, the audience is your active partner, often playing a role that you've chosen for them. With this in mind, you must learn to "open up." This term is often used by musical theater directors to refer to your body position vis-à-vis the audience, but it also refers more generally to an emotional openness that is required for successful singing-acting.

Going beyond what's "on the page." In Chapter 3, I invited you to think of yourself as not just a singer but also as a *creator*, the author of your performance. As a musical theater performer, you'll be adding details of behavior and expression to what's "on the page." Sometimes, this will come in conflict with the script, the stage directions and musical score, not to mention your notions of ideal vocal production. How much are you "allowed" to do to serve the higher cause of expressive, creative communication?

Mixing fixed and free elements. Many aspects of a musical theater performance get "set"—that is, decided on and determined—in rehearsal, and since so many elements are fixed, and the hierarchy of authority is so established, it can be hard to find and trust your real impulses to the point that you can improvise and create in the moment. Through training and experience, you must learn when you should "hit your marks" in rehearsal and performances and when you're free to "do your own thing." Live performance is created by real human beings doing real things in real time, and that means you've got to be alert and ready to respond to what's *really* happening. Unexpected things occur onstage, not just mistakes and flubs, but also magical moments that occur synergistically when creators and spectators come together. This is how art gets made. The studio is a great place to practice walking the tightrope between fixed and free elements on the musical stage.

Partner and ensemble considerations. When you share the stage with others during a musical, all sorts of special challenges present themselves. You have to maintain an illusion of spontaneity and believability while executing a score in which every decision about pitch, timing, loudness and inflection has already been agreed upon. Choreography, blocking, gestures and other types of physical behavior are often predetermined as well. The stage manager, the stagehands, the conductor and the musicians are counting on you to be consistent and predictable.

How do you keep your performance alive and authentic, not phony or mechanical, when confronted with this challenge? Group classes can be especially productive and effective for addressing this aspect of musical theater training, but there are other things you can do privately in the practice room to prepare yourself to work successfully in an ensemble.

Special Tools for Special Challenges

I've developed two distinctive and unique training tools to help you master these special sorts of challenges. They are a powerful part of the SAVI System: SAVI Études and SAVI Cards. Over the coming chapters, I'll make frequent references to both, so this would be a good time to introduce them.

SAVI Études. Throughout this book, you'll find a number of original exercises like "Here I Am," compositions I created to help my students master the fundamental challenges of singing acting. Since I'm a composer and lyricist as well as an educator, it felt natural to combine these two different creative activities in the pursuit of more effective ways to train singing actors in the classroom. These exercises are meant to be "rudimentary," designed to introduce basic principles in a way that invites mastery of fundamental skills. Many of these études are meant to be used in combination with SAVI Cards.

SAVI Cards. Years ago, back in the days when my sons were collecting Pokémon cards and baseball cards, I was inspired to experiment with collectible trading cards that could be used as part of the musical theater training experience. My discovery of the Oblique Strategies cards, created by Brian Eno and Peter Schmidt in 1975 to help artists and musicians be more creative, gave me encouragement to pursue this idea. SAVI Cards have proven to be remarkably effective as a **catalyst** for creative singing acting.

There are official SAVI Cards available as a companion to this book, and if you don't have them yet, I hope you will snag a set soon at savisingingactor.com. In the meantime, you're welcome to create some for yourself. The more personal and eccentric, the better. You can use index cards to make them or cut up sheets of paper into identically sized rectangles. Each card should contain a word, phrase, or picture that is meant to propose an idea or provoke a change in the course of an exercise or song.

SAVI Cards are an exciting way to supercharge a group class for musical theater performers. Exercises like the Mirror Canon (p. 108), Conducted Vocalese (p. 158), and the Three-Peat Echo Circle (p. 241) all take advantage of the rich dynamic of the group to support specific, varied choice-making. During group work, you or your teacher can divide up the cards among the group and encourage them to work in a way that is inspired by the word, instruction, or image on the card they currently hold. Pass the cards around to keep mixing things up. Calling out verbs, adjectives, or phrases from cards and handing cards to students during an exercise produce dramatic results.

But even if you are taking class regularly, it only lasts for an hour or two a week, and you need a way to continue to practice when you're on your own. The cards are especially useful in these circumstances. In what can easily become a sensorial void, SAVI Cards provide useful provocations that will inspire you to try an assortment of behaviors and actions on for size.

In short, SAVI Cards promote and support structured and specific choice-making. They focus your attention on a single, clearly defined choice for each phrase, and they invite you to discover the power and clarity that comes when you commit fully to a choice. They also promote variety as you practice switching from one card to the next at the moment a new phrase begins. In a warm-up or a workout, they provide a framework you can use to explore an array of choices, promoting range and flexibility in your behavioral life as a singing actor.

"Here I Am" with SAVI Cards

Combining SAVI Cards with the étude "Here I Am" is a powerful demonstration of the SAVI System at work. You might have noticed that this étude, with its pulsating accompaniment of triplets, induces a trancelike mood that may lead you toward generalized, undifferentiated behavior. The music for this étude is steady and unvaried in its texture, but that doesn't mean the behavior you create during the exercise should be that way. SAVI Cards give you a tool to explore what happens when you disrupt yourself and supply an "inner pinch" prior to the onset of the new phrase.

On page 36, the music is marked with a triangle at the moments where those opportunities for a change of behavior occur in the exercise. I call these triangles "dings." You'll see me to refer to them as such throughout this book; when I do, I am encouraging you to make a choice in your behavior actions. I'll provide the full 4-1-1 on "dings" in Chapter 6, but for now it's enough to know that "dings" often mean it's time for a new card.

Choose a couple cards from one or more categories of your SAVI Cards. (They have color-coded backs that make them easy to sort.) You can either spread them out in a row where you can see them all—the top of the piano or a music stand works great in a practice room—or hold them in a stack in your hand and flip through them one by one during the exercise.

Practice using a new card for every other ding, maintaining the choice on the card as you sing the second phrase with some slight adjustment or intensification. Then practice using a new card for every ding, or after a random number of dings. If you're handling the cards, flip to the new card and glance at it before the moment of the new ding occurs, so that you're ready to switch all at once to your new choice at the exact moment of the ding. Try working with a random sequence of cards where each new prompt comes as a surprise; for a different kind of experience, create and memorize a series of cards and then execute them in a planned sequence.

Your challenge while working with the cards is to **inhabit** every choice, that is, to commit fully to the choice presented on the card while making it feel like a spontaneous and authentic expression of your inner state. If the next card says "softer," find an emotional justification for singing softer. If the next card prompts you to play the action "to accuse," see if you can't find a way to make that action organic and believable even if you can't think of a logical reason why you'd begin singing in an accusatory manner.

There are eight different types of SAVI Cards in the Premier Edition set, and each one has its own special superpower:

- Action verbs prompt you to "do" something to your imaginary scene partner. The "reality of doing" is fundamental to believable behavior onstage.
- Adverbs describe *how* you do something, using your face, voice and body to truthfully express that quality.
- Emotions remind you of the full range of feelings you are capable of experiencing and prompt you to express them with your face, voice and body.
- Subtext cards prompt you to behave if these words were your unspoken thoughts.
- Pictures present faces and gestures to imitate and inspire you while you sing.
- Adjustments propose a change in how you're using your voice, face or body.
- Music and voice cards prompt you to change your vocal sound and musical interpretation.
- Custom cards give you a chance to create your own prompts, using words, phrases or pictures that have strong personal meaning.

SAVI Cards and SAVI Études are tools designed to help you hone your skills as a singing actor. They give you the ability to "work on the singer as well as the song," in the practice room as well as the classroom. I'll refer to them often in the chapters that follow. I invite you to think of them not just as *tools* but as *toys*, and play with them in a spirit of fearless curiosity.

CHAPTER 5

Training, Conditioning, Warming Up

If you want to attain peak performance as a singing actor, start by thinking of yourself as an athlete.

Musical theater performance is a demanding art form that requires you to be in top condition, not just vocally but also physically, mentally and emotionally. Especially in today's world of demanding, high-stakes musical theater performance, you need to take care of yourself like an athlete does. That means managing your lifestyle by eating well, staying hydrated, and getting enough sleep so that you're in peak performing condition. Peak performance can't be obtained with the occasional master class or a couple days of cramming; you need to organize your life much like an athlete does, making time for regular conditioning, skill development and application.

In this section, I'll help you identify the most important ways you can train yourself as a singing actor. We'll examine the gains you need to make vocally and physically and explore the activities that have proven to be most useful in cultivating a performer's singing-acting chops. Some of the most important work you will do every day in your training as a singing actor must take place before you can even begin to think about singing a song. In other words, you've got to "train to gain."

Think Like an Athlete

"Thinking like an athlete" may feel like a new concept to you; it largely depends on your previous experiences in dance, music, theater and athletics. If you started out as a dancer, an athlete or an instrumentalist, the idea is probably more familiar; in these fields of endeavor, it's more common to associate excellence with time and effort invested in training. If you came to musical theater having been a singer or actor first, you may not have had much contact with "training" outside of rehearsals for a show. Though it may be an unfamiliar concept, you'll find it has a great deal of validity.

In his 1938 book *The Theatre and Its Double*, actor and avant-garde director Antonin Artaud was the first to refer to actors as "athletes of the heart":

> We must recognize that the actor has a kind of emotional musculature that corresponds to certain physical localizations of feelings.
>
> The actor is like a real physical athlete, but with this surprising qualification, that he has an emotional organism that is analogous to the athlete's, which is parallel to it, which is like its double, although it does not operate on the same level.
>
> The actor is an athlete of the heart.[17]

With the publication of their 2014 book, *The Vocal Athlete*, Dr. Wendy LeBorgne and Marci Rosenberg brought the concept of elite athletic performance to the world of singing. LeBorgne and Rosenberg recognized that vocalists attempting extreme feats, such as singing high, loud, with strong emotion, for prolonged periods of time, require extreme skills to achieve peak performance, and that the proper training regimen can reduce their risk of injury or trauma.

---

[17] Antonin Artaud, "An Emotional Athleticism," in *Antonin Artaud: Selected Writings* (Berkeley: University of California Press, 1988), 259-60.

Singers and musicians are more accustomed to thinking of "practicing" rather than "training," but I like the athletic connotations of words like "training" and "conditioning." For some musicians, "practicing" is an activity that focuses almost exclusively on repertoire, but truly effective practicing includes technique work in addition to repertoire study. You'd never want to hear scales and exercises in a concert, but time spent playing technical studies like these develops both physical and mental capabilities that you'll need when it's time to begin work on specific pieces.

The Best Ways to Train

The athlete is a useful model to have as you head off to the practice room to start working with your SAVI Cards. With this in mind, let's talk for a minute about the best ways to train and to practice. We've all heard the saying "Practice makes perfect," but practice is only effective when it's done *deliberately*. This means:

- Practicing persistently, making it a habit;
- Practicing purposefully, with specific goals in mind and a plan to challenge yourself;
- Getting frequent informed feedback, so you know how you're doing and can correct mistakes before they become bad habits.

Persistence. If you want to make progress, you've got to put in the time. When you rehearse, you're getting ready for opening night, but you're not necessarily building the complete set of skills you need to succeed in every show. To do that, you must train the way an athlete, a dancer or an instrumental musician trains—that is, working deliberately and patiently on the rudiments and the fundamental skills that your chosen field of endeavor requires.

To practice persistently, I recommend you schedule your practice sessions and track your efforts. It's also a big help to have a designated place to go, a familiar spot where you'll have the materials you need and where you won't have to worry about privacy or being interrupted. Track your practicing using a journal or a chart like the one you'll find at the end of this workbook. At the beginning of each week, make a plan about when and where you'll practice, and at the end of the week, review the efforts you've recorded in your practice tracker. With this feedback in mind, you can make informed decisions about how you want to adjust your practicing for the following week.

A sense of purpose. To practice productively, it's helpful to begin your practice sessions with specific goals in mind, as well as a plan of action for reaching those goals.

An optimal practice session begins with a 10- to 20-minute warm-up and includes time spent on at least three different sorts of activities:

- Conditioning: building skills and mastering rudiments, pushing against the limits of your abilities to build range, strength, flexibility, coordination and stamina;
- Exploring: investigating a greater range of possibilities you can bring to exercises and repertoire;
- Crafting: identifying the best choices for the repertoire you're preparing, and strengthening your ability to execute those choices reliably.

A good practice log or chart will provide a designated place to track the time you spent on each of these activities in your sessions, as I've done in the example below.

DATE TIME	Monday [write down start and end times]	Tuesday	Wednesday	(and so on)
Warm-up	10 minutes			
Conditioning	How long? What exercises and activities did you do?			
Exploring	How long? What did you do? What seemed useful? Frustrating?			
Crafting	How long? What did you do?			
Video Feedback	What did you record? What did it help you see?			
Notes	Are you preparing for anything in particular? What pieces? How'd it go? What would you like to try next time?			

Feedback. Getting prompt and frequent feedback is a little bit trickier when you're a singing actor. This is because you are your own instrument, and it's counterproductive to observe yourself while you're practicing. Evaluating your success at creating behavior requires you to be able to hear and see what you're doing and examine it with a cool head, without letting the excitement and pressure of performance interfere with your perceptions and judgment.

Of course, that's what a teacher, coach or director does for you, but nowadays, there's another option available. Casual video, shot using your phone, tablet or camera, can give you the objective perspective you need to evaluate your work. Get a little tripod to set up your device with a good view of where you're working. It's better NOT to have the screen facing you, since it's sure to distract and inhibit you while you're working. Make it your habit to capture some recorded footage for at least one part of every practice session, and assess your progress by watching what you recorded. I've included a place on my practice log chart, above, to encourage you track whether or not you did that.

Self-recording will never fully replace the expert feedback you can get from a teacher or coach. Those specialists have knowledge and insight that enable them to evaluate what you're doing thoughtfully and efficiently and make recommendations based on their own training and experience. Still, you can make meaningful progress on the days when you don't have a class or lesson by using self-recording as a tool for self-evaluation. What's more, you always have the option of sharing your video with an off-site coach or teacher to get their informed comments.

Components of an Effective Warm-Up

A good warm-up gets every part of your instrument ready to work. As a singing actor, you'll use your face, body and mind to express yourself, and a good warm-up will help to activate and energize every part of you needed for that endeavor, including:

- The muscles of **_respiration_** (breath);

- The muscles and organs used in **phonation** (production of sound);
- The parts of your body that create **resonance** (amplification of vowel sounds);
- The muscles of **articulation** (diction);
- The muscles of the face used in the expression of emotion;
- The muscles around the eye that control focus and gaze;
- The use of the entire body in expressive movement, gesture and stance;
- Your "sixth sense" of **proprioception** that provides an awareness of what your body is doing, including your posture, your alignment and your vocal mechanism.

Increasing vitality and ease and reducing any stiffness or excess tension that may inhibit or distort these muscles and other physical attributes should be an important goal during your warm-up.

The 8-Step SAVI Warm-Up

Here are 8 types of activities for you to include in warm-up, along with ideas about how to use SAVI Cards to enhance these activities. Spend a minute or two on each activity for a total of 10 to 20 minutes at the beginning of each practice session or rehearsal, and you'll be rewarded with greater expressiveness and ease!

1. **Breathing**. Good breathing is not only the foundation of good singing, but it also affects your emotional and physical state. The goal of a breathing warm-up should be to stretch, activate and strengthen the muscles of respiration so that you can breathe dynamically. You also want to practice coordinating the movements of the abdomen, diaphragm and ribcage required for effective inhalation and regulation of airflow during phonation.

RECOMMENDED ACTIVITIES:

- Inhaling through a straw or through tightly pursed lips, "sipping" the air through a constricted opening that creates resistance.

- Alternate nostril breathing: cover one nostril with your thumb and breathe in through the other. Then, open the covered nostril, close the opposite nostril with your ring finger, and breathe out. Repeat as needed.

- Hissing, both with a steady stream or while pulsing the breath.

- Panting, first without phonation, then with vocal sound on the exhalation.

- Short "huhs" and "heys," using abdominal muscles for accents, followed by sustained sounds with steady abdominal contraction.

- Slow, regulated exhalation while counting or intoning on a narrow pitch range.

USING THE CARDS: Use the SAVI Cards in your breathing warm-up to cultivate the integration of breath and dramatic imagination. The emotion cards, adjective cards and dramatic action cards all suggest potentially useful qualities to explore.

In *The Theater and Its Double*, Artaud writes, "every feeling, every mental action, every leap of human emotion… [has a] corresponding breath."[18] Later, he adds, "Breath accompanies the feeling, and one can penetrate into the feeling by the breath, provided one has been able to discriminate which one corresponds to what feeling." Let the SAVI Cards inspire you as you explore the relationship between feeling and breath during the first part of your warm-up.

2. Vocal play. Once the breath is flowing, you're ready to warm up your "vocal instrument." This part of the warm-up will probably seem familiar; it typically includes ***vocalises***, musical

---

[18] Antonin Artaud, *The Theater and Its Double*, translated by Mary Caroline Richards (New York: Grove Press, 1958), 134.

patterns of pitched vowel sounds like the ones you've learned in voice lessons and chorus rehearsals. Your goal in this part of the warm-up is to fully activate your organs of phonation and optimize your use of the parts of your body where you create resonance. You will use your senses of hearing and proprioception to guide you as you explore a full range of pitch, volume and vocal qualities.

RECOMMENDED ACTIVITIES:

- "Lip trill" sounds: Like the "brr" sound you make when you're cold, this is a pitched sound you make as you push air through loose lips. Glide or "siren" your pitch up and down.
- Closed-mouth sounds (*mm, nn* and *ng*) and voiced consonant sounds (*v, z, zh, th* and *r*), with a gliding pitch up and down.
- Exercises that include all 12 **monophthongs**, the single-vowel sounds common in spoken and sung English. A mnemonic that will help you recall all 12 of these sounds is, "Who would know aught of art must learn, act, and then take his ease." I've set this phrase to a simple melody that works well in a warm-up:

- Try glides, "sirening" up and down on all vowel sounds and closed-mouth sounds.
- Glides and melodies sung through a soda straw. Dr. Ingo Titze is the vocal scientist who has

popularized the use of straw phonation; check it out online![19]

- Vocalises: If you're taking voice lessons, your vocal teacher has probably recommended vocalises for you to use in a warm-up. If you sing in a choir, you've probably done vocalises at the beginning of rehearsal.

USING THE CARDS: Use the SAVI Cards in your vocal warm-up to broaden your palette of qualities, dynamic choices and "vocal behaviors." Have your cards handy while you vocalize, and choose one or two at a time to stimulate your dramatic imagination while you're making sound.

3. Face and eyes. The face is your most powerful "organ of expression," but few of us use it to its full potential. Look at all the muscles shown on the illustration below! There are more than 300 muscles in the face, and learning to activate them use them in an articulate, expressive way is possibly the most productive thing you can do to improve your singing performance. For starters, this means making sure those muscles are strong and flexible, and that you're not inhibited by tension or a fear of looking foolish. Remember, it's no disgrace to use your face! With time and training, your facial proprioceptors will grow more sensitive. As a result, you'll have a clearer sense of what your face and eyes are doing even if you can't see yourself in a mirror or on a video monitor.

---

[19] Julia Belluz, "How Blowing into a Straw Can Save Your Voice," *Vox*, June 20, 2015, www.vox.com/2015/6/20/8816065/how-not-to-lose-your-voice.

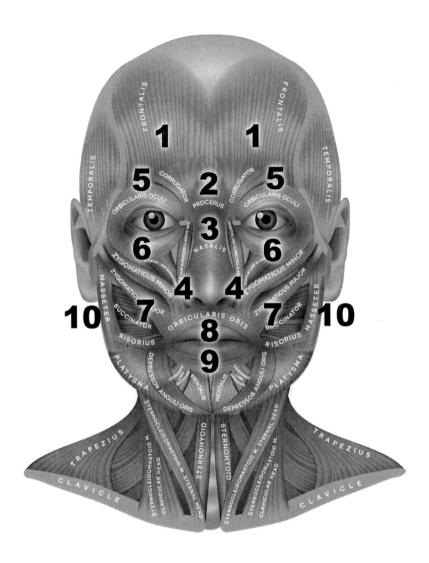

RECOMMENDED ACTIVITIES: Here are some of my favorite warm-up activities for the face and eyes.

- "Facial Flex": Flex and stretch the muscles in the different regions of your face, including the forehead; the **corrugator** muscle (between your eyebrows, it contracts when you scowl); the nose and nostrils; the muscles above and below the eyes;

the muscles of the cheeks (the strap-like **zygo-matic** muscles that are used when you smile); the lips; the jaw (moving it both up and down and from side to side); and the muscles of the **occipital region** (rocking and tilting the head gently on the atlas, the first cervical vertebra of the spine).

- Gurning: Great Britain has a tradition called **gurning**, in which people compete to see who can make the most extreme, grotesque faces. (If you don't believe me, Google it!) To warm up your face, you gotta gurn, baby, gurn!
- Muscles around the Eyes: Make yourself blink, wink and squint. Widen your eyes without raising your eyebrows, if possible. Squeeze your eyes tightly shut and hold for a count of five, then open your eyes wide and hold for a count of five.
- Muscles that Control the Movement of the Eyes: Look left, right, up, down. Move your eyes around like you are tracking a flying insect without moving your head. Focus on something far away, then something close. Look at an object with a soft focus, then a sharp focus.
- "Lazy Eights": Extend your arm and hold your thumb up in front of your face. In the air in front of you, draw a figure eight on its side (like the symbol for infinity, ∞), tracking your thumb with your gaze. Practice with both arms and in both directions.
- "One-Two" Focus Shifts: All at once, shift your gaze from one place to another. A moment later, adjust the position of your head so that you're facing the thing you're gazing at. The "one-two" focus shift is described more fully later in this workbook, along with an étude you can use to work on this key skill.

USING THE CARDS: The SAVI Face Cards are especially useful in warming up the face and eyes. Hold a Face Card up at arm's length and make your face match what you see on the card. Try doing this in front of a mirror—first using the muscles of your face to match the picture on the card you're looking at, then lowering the card and looking at your face in the mirror. You can also use the Adjective and Emotion Cards to inspire expressive face making and the Phrase Cards as an inner monologue you can practice conveying through the use of your face and eyes.

4. **Neck and alignment.** In this part of the warm-up, your goal is to make sure that your head, neck and spine are optimally aligned, with your head balanced on top of your spine and your posture not slumped, slouched or needlessly rigid. The study of Alexander Technique, which focuses on undoing unnecessary tension and collapse, is an ideal way to enhance awareness of your alignment and optimize your use of physical effort.

RECOMMENDED ACTIVITIES:

- Roll down the spine to touch your toes. Shake it out, then curl up slowly (vertebra by vertebra)
- Neck rolls with a relaxed jaw
- Gentle nodding movement made using an imaginary rod running through your ears as a pivot
- Gentle tilting movements made by lowering one ear toward the shoulder, then the other
- Gentle rotation of the head atop the spine by shaking your head "no"

Please note: a vigorous use of the voice in Part 2 or the facial muscles in Part 3 of your warm-up may cause your alignment to become distorted, including a "forward translation" of the head. Try to maintain an optimal relationship among the head, neck and upper body while warming up the face and voice.

*Energizing the face can result in a
forward translation of the skull, as seen here.*

5. **Articulators**. The coordinated, dynamic use of your lips, tongue, teeth and soft palate is required for clear, compelling diction when you speak and sing. If you want to use these articulators effectively, you'll need to move the muscles of the face more dynamically than you usually do. Review the consonant chart above to see the full range of consonants and the parts of the body used to make them. Your performance will be enhanced when you pay attention to the muscles and surfaces involved in articulation as you warm up.

RECOMMENDED ACTIVITIES:

- Be attentive to your articulators even in your vocal and facial warm-ups (Steps 2 and 3).

- Tongue Stretches: Lower the jaw and leave it lowered as you extend and retract the tongue.
- Mouth and Jaw Stretches: Speak with a wine cork or a carrot stick between your teeth.
- "Muppet Mouth" (Jaw Swings): Say "blah blah blah" or "flah flah flah" with an exaggerated movement of the jaw.
- Tongue Twisters: You know these already. "The tip of the tongue, the teeth, the lips," etc.
- Add initial and/or final consonants to your vocalises: "may mee mah moe moo," "zay zee zah," "vay vee vah," "Zhay zhee zhee" and so on.
- Vocalise with final consonants and shadow vowels: "Unique New York."

USING THE CARDS: The SAVI Phrase Cards can be used to practice diction and articulation. When you apply Action, Adjective and Emotion Cards to practice songs, you may find that a heightened awareness of diction can play a major role in expressing the actions and emotions on the cards.

6. Gesture and movement. A comprehensive warm-up should include work on the body in addition to work on the breath, voice, face and eyes. Your warm-up should increase blood flow, stretch tight muscles, free up your joints and create a sense of vitality and buoyancy in your body.

RECOMMENDED ACTIVITIES:

- Simple cardiovascular warm-ups: run in place, do jumping jacks, bounce on your toes.

- Shake out like a ragdoll or a wet dog.
- Move and dance like a marionette with very loose joints.

- All sorts of dancing. Play some music and get yourself moving!

USING THE CARDS: The SAVI Gesture Cards (body, face, partner and space) can be effectively combined with the phrases of your vocalises to prompt different sorts of gestures while you sing.

Movement in the space. There's no need to confine yourself to a single spot in the room or on the stage when you sing, and the same is true of your warm-up. In your warm-up, your goal should be to remind yourself of the kinds of expressiveness available to you when you move around the space.

RECOMMENDED ACTIVITIES: Walkabout, changing direction, tempo or quality of your movement on a "ding" signal if you are working with a teacher or partner. If you are working alone, count to 10 and then change direction, tempo or quality of movement.

USING THE CARDS: Perform your walkabout with an Adjective Card, an Action Verb card, an Emotion Card or a Phrase

Card serving as your inner monologue. Modify the movement with Quality cards.

8. Combining voice with focus, facial expression and movement. Finally, it is time to "put it together," combining your warmed-up voice and face with your eye and body movements. Use the SAVI Cards to stimulate your dramatic imagination as you vocalize.

If and when possible, this can be a great activity to spend an extended period of time on. As you extend your "warm-up time" (getting ready to practice) into "practice time" (purposefully conditioning and building skills), you'll grow increasingly accustomed to making different behavioral choices with each vocal phrase, and to coordinating your transition from one choice to the next with the specific moment in the music where one phrase is ending and the next is beginning.

SUMMARY: 8 WARM-UP ACTIVITIES

	Goals	Cards (Emotions, Adjectives, Action Verbs, Faces, Phrases, Music & Voice, Gesture and Quality, "Dings," Secrets)	Notes
Breath	Stretch, activate and strengthen muscles for more dynamic use of breath; practice coordination of abdominal release and diaphragmatic contraction	Use all cards to cultivate a combination of breath and dramatic imagination	Breathe with straw Alternate nostril breathing Panting Hissing with pulse "Huhs" using abdominal muscles for accents
Vocal play	Stimulate phonation and resonance; explore range of vocal behaviors	Use all cards to explore range, timbre, dynamics	Closed-mouth sounds (mm, nn, ng) Lip trill sounds Open mouth sounds: all vowels expressed first legato, then staccato Scales, arpeggios, vocalises
Face and eyes	Stretch and activate muscles of the face and eyes; practice conscious movement of eyes and focal shift; explore connection among face, eyes and emotion	Use Face Cards as models to imitate; other cards as catalysts for expression in face and eyes ("thinking eye")	Facial flex, gurn all zones including lips, jaw Muscles around eyes: blink, wink, squint, widen Eye movements: up/down, left/right, "Lazy Eight" Soft and hard focus, distant and close focus "One-two" focus shift
Neck and alignment	Stretch, activate muscles of occipital region, spine, pelvis		Neck roll Roll down and curl up Nod, tilt, head shake Facial flex with free neck
Articulators	Promote strong, clear and expressive diction	Text Cards	Tongue stretch Tongue twisters
Gesture and movement	Promote vitality, ease, impulsiveness, variety of available choices	Gesture Cards (face, space, body, partner)	Cardio: Jumping jacks, ragdoll "Wet dog," marionette dance Free play of gesture
Movement in space	Awaken awareness of space and potential for movement	Action, Adjective, Phrases (as inner monologue)	Walkabout, change tempo, direction, quality with dings Movement with music
Voice and eyes	Coordinate singing and focus	All cards (one per phrase)	Pre-select and memorize card(s) to eliminate the need to look at cards during exercise
Voice and face	Coordinate vocal and facial expression	Especially Face Cards	Remain alert to potential for distortion of alignment
Voice, gesture and movement	Coordinate and integrate singing with gesture and movement	All cards (one per phrase)	Cards can be pre-selected and memorized, laid out in sequence, held by practice buddy or held in hand and flipped prior to ding

CHAPTER 6

Working Phrase by Phrase

The concept of working "phrase by phrase" is one of the most fundamental and powerful tools of SAVI singing-acting. Every phrase has three parts: a beginning, a middle, and an end, each of which requires particular skills that can be enhanced through practice. The importance of the moment when a phrase begins cannot be overemphasized; in SAVI speak, this is called "the ding." In this chapter, you'll learn more about the anatomy of a phrase and how to "sing and ding." The exercises in this chapter give you opportunities to work on individual phrases in isolation and develop the skills you'll need to build and execute a sequence of phrases.

What is a Phrase?

The word "phrase" is used by writers, musicians and dancers to refer to the building blocks of their creative expression. A **phrase** is a series of words, sounds and/or movements with a distinct collective identity and function. It is a self-contained unit of meaning and expression, capable of being understood even when isolated from the larger work of which it is a part. A song is a sequence of phrases—that is, a series of individual events made up of text, music and (in performance) behavior. It is crafted by the writer, composer and performer to create a structured progression or journey, often with a discernable design, a meaningful relationship between the whole work and its component parts, and a sense of completion at the end. Used as a verb, "to phrase" describes the act of performing in a way that pays careful attention to the distinctive shape and character of each individual unit of expression and its place in the progression of the complete work.

We tend to think of a song as a single thing, often associating the overall dramatic event and the characteristic musical features of the song with its title. This is not surprising, since that unifying quality is a fundamental consideration in the design and structure of a song. A typical song begins with an introduction, builds to a climax and ends with some sort of audible signal (the so-called **button**) that the song is complete. Between intro and button, a song uses repetition, rhyme, rhythm, pattern and other structural devices to create the impression that it has been wrought from a series of connected, compelling ideas in a way that gives it impact and makes it memorable.

Though a song may seem singular and unified to the listener or spectator, the singer must present the journey of the song one phrase at a time. This concept is at the heart of Axiom 7:

A song must be understood and presented as a journey, a series of events that occur in sequence. Navigating the "journey of the song" is like following turn-by-turn directions.

In a song, words and music usually work in tandem, shaping the expression of thoughts and feelings into a sequence that can be quite short–sometimes no more than a single syllable–or quite long. A phrase can be simple or complex; it can be a direct declarative statement or an elaborate construction with dependent clauses, linked lists and parenthetical digressions. A phrase that lasts longer than 10 seconds (a dozen syllables or more at a moderate tempo) is a very long phrase indeed, and can challenge the listener's comprehension or attention span. A typical phrase, though, is just a handful of syllables with a clear singular function.

Recognizing the beginnings and ends of the phrases in your song may be complicated by the fact that the phrases of the *lyric* don't always have a neat one-to-one correspondence to the phrases of the *music*. Sometimes a single phrase of music can contain more than one phrase of text, and sometimes a long sentence of text can span several phrases of music before the idea is fully expressed. Here's a SAVI suggestion: when they differ, phrase with the lyric. The lyric is always your most reliable indication of when a phrase is complete or a new one has begun.

Moment-to-Moment is NOT Phrase-by-Phrase

Acting teacher Sanford Meisner talks about the importance of "living in the moment" and working "moment to moment." A moment is, by definition, something quite brief, almost instantaneous. A moment occurs any time we choose to open our senses and notice what's happening *now*, and there are an infinite number of "now's" available for us to notice. Being alert to these "now's" is a key ingredient of Authenticity, and being able to live "in the moment" means actively noticing and processing the information that floods in through our senses in real time.

I think of all those moments, those "now's" as grains of sand that flow through an hourglass, one after another in a continuous "stream of consciousness," a concept introduced by psychologist William James and employed so effectively in James Joyce's *Ulysses*.

In a song, however, those moments have been organized into a series of phrases to create impact. Moments are granular, but phrases are "chunks," each of which has a particular shape, weight and duration. Composer John Kander, speaking on behalf of his late lyricist partner, Fred Ebb, offered this advice to my friend Forrest McClendon when he was rehearsing for the premiere production of *The Scottsboro Boys*: "Whatever you do, *put over* that lyric." Kander's use of the phrase "put over," an old-fashioned bit of showbiz parlance, suggests that a lyric is like a projectile that must get past some sort of barrier to reach its target. When a song is successfully "put over," it has impact, and the phrases are said to "land" on the listener, like something dropped from above.

A phrase, then, contains many moments: the moments that precede the initial impulse, when the phrase is imminent but not yet inevitable; the impulsive moment when you decide to begin the phrase; the ensuing moments when you are carried along by the "momentum" of your initial impulse; the moments when you are aware of something or someone responding to you; and finally, the moment when you've fulfilled your mission and there's nothing left to say.

John Bucchino's marvelous art song "This Moment" is composed of a series of one- and two-word phrases that convey the wonder and exhilaration of living moment to moment. This song is a unique example in which each brief phrase is its own moment. Apart from the rare exception, though, the terms "moment to moment" and "phrase by phrase" are not interchangeable. Whether you're singing, speaking, or silent, you must learn to live truthfully in each and every moment while remaining attentive to the way the songwriter has organized those moments into "chunks"-phrases and stanzas and verses-that deliver information and emotion with beauty, order and impact.

Beginning, Middle, and End

Whether short or long, each phrase in a song has a beginning, a middle and an end, and each of those three constituent parts has distinctive characteristics.

Whether you're working on SAVI exercises or songs, make it your goal to increase your ability to:

- begin a phrase impulsively;
- sustain and develop that impulse with no more effort than necessary for the duration of the middle; and
- release tension and effort at the end of the phrase to clear the way for the next one to begin and for the cycle to repeat.

Let's examine these three different components of a phrase and what they mean to you as a singing actor.

Beginning. I often refer to the beginning of a phrase as its *onset*. A phrase begins with a distinct impulse, launched with an energy or force that comes from intention. The thought or idea that animates the phrase and provides the source of its energy usually occurs a moment before the phrase begins. Once that idea has triggered the impulse to speak (or sing), it is quickly, almost instantly, followed by an intake of breath. Only then can the singing start.

Idea ----> Intake of breath ----> Sound

It may be helpful to think of a phrase as an "ouch" that must be preceded by a "pinch." ("Pinch and ouch" is a phrase you may recognize from Sanford Meisner's acting pedagogy.) The pinch, the initial impulse that leads to the phrase, may be a literal pinch (a bit of physical discomfort inflicted by your partner); the behavioral equivalent of a pinch (your partner says or does something that triggers you); or an inner pinch (you suddenly recall something or figure something out). In each of these three cases, the "pinch-y" quality of the initial idea is sharp and sudden, and the intake of breath is almost instantaneous, quickly followed by the vocal phrase and its accompanying behavior: "Ouch!" "Aha!" "Hey!"

Middle. The middle of the phrase requires a different kind of energy than its beginning. The middle is when your initial impulse "blooms" into a verbal, musical and behavioral expression that can last for many seconds. The middle of a phrase is like the moments when an arrow is in flight between bow and target. Unlike an arrow in flight, you're still in control of a phrase when you're in the middle of it, but it's best to use no more effort than necessary to sustain, guide and develop the middle of the phrase. The initial launch of a phrase is energy-intensive, but during the middle, you can take advantage of the momentum created by that initial burst of energy.

End. The end of a phrase is like the moment you see in old war movies, where the radioman concludes his message by saying, "Over!", which means, "I'm done speaking, and now it's your turn." Approaching the end of the phrase, your attention shifts from output to input. You take in new information from your real or imaginary partner.

Whatever you were "doing" to your partner during the phrase, now's the time to determine whether you successfully "did" it. If you asked a question, give your partner a chance to respond; if you confessed your feelings, see what your partner's reaction is. During this part of the phrase, it's helpful to get in the habit of releasing the muscles that were involved in starting and sustaining the phrase as fully as you can. Incorporating a conscious "floppy release" at the end of a phrase creates more ideal conditions for taking in the sensory information you need to make an adjustment and start the next phrase. (In Chapter 11, I'll have more to say about the importance of "coming to your senses" and the role of sensory input in successful singing acting.)

But unless you've sung the last phrase of the song, your work isn't done yet. A new pinch-perhaps a response from your partner, a lack of response from your partner, or a new thought or impulse to modify or add on to what you just said-will trigger a new phrase, and the AAA Cycle (described earlier) will repeat itself.

EXERCISE: Short-Phrase Études

Here is a short exercise that provides a great opportunity for you to work on how you should approach the beginning, middle and end of a phrase.

"Get Away From Me" is an exercise that can be done with either a real or an imaginary partner. When you sing this, imagine a threat approaching. Your impulse to sing should come from the urge to stop this menacing intruder. The middle of the phrase is delivered with focused force and urgency; the language uses the imperative mood (a command expressed in a sentence with no subject); and the music is tense and rhythmic, with only a repeated single pitch in the melody.

At the end of the phrase, the exercise requires you to make a quick transition from acting upon your menacing partner to noticing their response to your command. Did you succeed in stopping the intruder or are you still in danger? If the latter is what you see, modulate up a half step and repeat the phrase. This is the Triple-A Cycle in action: Act, then Assess, then Adjust.

"Come to Me" is another good exercise to practice with a partner, then alone, focusing on the different approaches required for the beginning, middle and end of the phrase. You can also try making up your own tunes for any of the short phrases on the SAVI Subtext Cards.

Anatomy of a Long Phrase

As previously stated, phrases can be short or long. Despite its unusual length (34 syllables, just over 20 seconds long), this passage from Gilbert and Sullivan's *The Pirates of Penzance* is a good example of a lengthy single phrase.

Oh, is there not one maiden breast
Which does not feel the moral beauty
Of making worldly interest
Subordinate to sense of duty?

Let's take a moment to admire how this single question, this single unit of thought and expression, is elegantly constructed from a set of interrelated verbal and musical motifs. Its pieces fit together elegantly to make a well-organized whole, giving it both unity and variety.

Like all phrases, this one has a beginning, a middle, and an end. It begins with a question from a young man looking for a young woman interested in being dutiful even if it means forgo-ing "worldly" pleasures. Though it takes him nearly half a minute to describe the sort of woman he's looking for, he holds the ques-tion fully formed in his mind the whole time he sings it. He can't let his attention wander or his behavior distract us in the middle of the phrase. Otherwise, we'll lose the thread of his argument before he gets to the subject of "duty," the thing that matters most to him.

As he reaches the end of his question, the singer must focus his attention on the young women he is singing to. In the operetta, Frederic sings to a chorus of young maidens to see if an answer to his question is forthcoming. He switches from "output mode" (describing what he's looking for) to "input mode" (assessing the reaction of his listeners). *Are you the girl I'm looking for?* he thinks to himself as he looks at each one in turn. *What about you? Am I frightening you? Am I being clear?* In the last few beats before the next phrase begins, he must make a judgment based on the girls' unspoken response. Then, he begins a new stanza that asks a new question.

It requires stamina and control to execute a long, complex phrase like this, much less have it understood as a single unit of action and expression. The chief skill required here is the ability to recognize when a new thought is beginning and to only make a behavioral adjustment at the start of a phrase, not in the middle of one. If you fail to recognize the onset of a new thought, you'll sail right past a transition like a driver missing a turn. Alternatively, you might make an unnecessary turn at a moment when continu-ing in the same direction is the appropriate choice. Learning to exert self-control and to navigate the journey of the song phrase by phrase will give your singing greater meaning and expression.

It Don't Mean a Thing...

> It don't mean a thing
> If it ain't got that "ding."
>> – With apologies to Duke Ellington and Irving Mills

In order to work "phrase by phrase," you need to understand where each new phrase begins. In SAVI talk, that's the **ding**, the onset of the new musical, lyrical or movement-based idea in the piece.

The topic of song analysis is an important one in SAVI Singing Acting, and is considered much more thoroughly in the section of the book that starts with Chapter 12: "Work on the Song." As we "work on the singer" in these chapters, though, we'll need to refer occasionally to songs to provide explicit illustrations of some of the challenges the singing actor typically faces. I want to use a brief example here to illustrate "dings," and I've chosen to use a short excerpt of an original song called "I'll Be Known." You can find it in its entirety in Chapter 12. If you want to know more about this song and the show it comes from, by all means, jump ahead and take a look before we proceed.

Now that you're back, let's start by taking a look at the lyrics:

> I want to be heard,
> I want to be seen.
> I want to be noticed,
> Do you know what I mean?
> I want to be known.

This is a five-line **stanza**, the term songwriters and poets use to refer to a group of lines or phrases arranged in a pattern that will recur throughout the composition. In this example, the lyric is laid out on the page so that each line is a separate phrase, but that's not always the case. Learning to identify where each phrase begins is an important skill for successful singing-acting, since each new phrase presents a unique opportunity for specific expression or communication. We'll dive into that challenge in greater depth in Chapter 13.

In order to unlock the power of phrase-by-phrase interpretation, start by marking the spot in the musical score or the lyric sheet where each phrase begins. In the SAVI System, we use a triangle to mark the ding:

Δ   I want to be heard,
Δ   I want to be seen.
Δ   I want to be noticed,
Δ   Do you know what I mean?
Δ   I want to be known.

Why a triangle? It's the symbol for the Greek letter **delta**, which is used in the world of science and math to denote change. A triangle is also a musical instrument whose sound is a distinctive "ding." And maybe you noticed that it appears in the middle of the SAVI logo, as seen on the cover of this book.

Later, in Chapter 13, I'll explore the topic of song analysis much more extensively; if you're eager to dig into that subject or have a song you want to prepare right now, by all means, skip ahead! However, it's equally important we focus on you, the singer, as well as the song. The technical skill of making specific behavioral choices for each phrase and transitioning cleanly from one phrase to the next–what in SAVI talk we call your ability to "sing and ding"–can be practiced apart from the work you do to prepare any given song for performance.

EXERCISE: I Have a New Idea

The étude "I Have a New Idea" is a three-phrase musical composition. The first two phrases are just one measure long, while the third is two measures long.

Perhaps it's unclear why I divide the first half of the exercise into two short phrases instead of treating it a single two-measure phrase. Even though it is not a complete sentence, "a thought I must explain" is a separate phrase prompted by an impulse to explain the nature of the "idea" named in the first phrase. These two phrases operate as a kind of "linked pair," where the impulse for the second phrase originates in the first phrase. Try singing "I have a new idea," treating "idea" as the end of a phrase and taking in sensory information from your partner before making a slight behavioral adjustment as you initiate "a thought I must explain." See below for more on "conjoined" or "linked phrases."

Notice that the third phrase of "I Have a New Idea" is twice as long as the first two. It begins with a comma and a linking word ("and"), clearly separating it from its predecessor. As you sing the étude "I Have a New Idea," pay attention to the beginnings of the phrases, the impulses that activate each phrase in turn, and the different amounts of energy required to sustain a one- or a two-measure phrase.

EXERCISE: (I Can) Ding and Sing

Being the clever reader you are, you've no doubt figured out by now that a phrase is the thing that happens between two dings. The ding, where one phrase ends and the next one begins, is an instantaneous moment of change, and change creates meaning. Learning to "sing and ding" is the most effective way I've found to increase Specificity and Variety, and that's what this next exercise, "Ding and Sing," was created to do.

If "Here I Am" is the power ballad of SAVI études, then "Ding and Sing" is its up-tempo number, a SAVI "bop." "Ding and Sing" presents the same technical challenges and opportunities as the previous exercise but with a livelier musical setting.

A word of warning: Both the ballad and the bop come with built-in temptations to generalize—that is, to make performance choices based on the general feeling and tempo of the music without taking into account the specific moments in the song where one phrase ends and the next begins. The lively gospel-style accompaniment of "Ding and Sing" is fun and uplifting, but your responsibility remains the same: to create behavior that communicates the dramatic event, phrase by phrase.

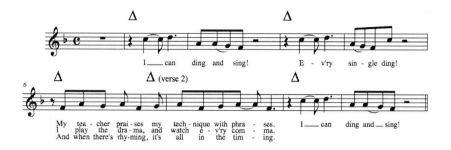

When you're first learning "Ding and Sing," you want to practice coordinating the behavioral adjustments that occur on the down-beat of measures 2, 4, 6 and 8 with singing the lyric. (Verse 2 comes with its own special challenge, since there's an additional ding (and an additional adjustment to make) after "drama.")

To help students remember to do this in a classroom situation, I use an audible signal at each ding. The sound of the triangle works well for this, but playing it requires two hands, so I often use a "desk bell," the sort of thing you'd find on a hotel reception desk or a store counter. A brisk tap on the top button produces a piercing "ding" sound that gets everyone's attention in a hurry. Giving one student the task of sounding the bell while the others sing and execute the exercise reinforces their understanding of the importance of timing the dings correctly with the music.

Once the coordination of singing and behavior adjustments has been mastered, it's time to associate more specific behavioral choices with each phrase of the song, and that's your cue to get out your SAVI Cards. Each verse in "Ding and Sing" needs four cards (except for Verse 2, which needs five). Choose cards for one verse and lay them out where you can see them with an indirect glance; you don't want to disrupt the exercise with a long look at the cards to see what's next.

It is a good idea to start practicing "Ding and Sing" slowly and mechanically before bringing your work up to a performance-level energy and tempo. You might also consider working on the phrases in reverse order. Begin with the final phrase and find a strong behavioral statement to accompany it; repeat that phrase until your choice is "set." Next, back up to the penultimate phrase and make some sort of contrasting behavioral choice for it. How will that choice flow into your choice for the final phrase? Practice the transition between the second-to-last phrase and the final phrase, and then repeat the two-phrase sequence until you can execute it confidently. Then go back to the third-from-last phrase and repeat the process, creating a three-phrase sequence, then once more to practice the full song. If it helps to have a visual aid, here's what each step would look like:

Final Phrase.	Δ	I can ding and sing!
Last 2 Phrases.	Δ	My teacher praises my technique with phrases.
	Δ	I can ding and sing!
Last 3 Phrases.	Δ	Every single ding!
	Δ	My teacher praises my technique with phrases.
	Δ	I can ding and sing!
All 4 Phrases.	Δ	I can ding and sing!
	Δ	Every single ding!
	Δ	My teacher praises my technique with phrases.
	Δ	I can ding and sing!

Alternate between "marking" the phrases—executing the behavior fully but lightly with little or no singing voice—and giving them "full-out" performance energy, and use plenty of repetitions to create this routine.

"Ding and Sing" with SAVI Cards

The étude "Ding and Sing" offers another great opportunity to work with your SAVI Cards. Select four cards and lay them out in a random order. Each time you get to the next "ding," use one of the four cards to prompt a new behavior choice. For instance, try using one example of each category of gesture–body, face, partner and space–in the four phrases of the exercise.

Try to inhabit each of your choices and endow them with as much meaning and authentic truth as you can. After practicing for a little while, use the video camera in your phone or laptop to record your work, then take a look and see what you think. Does your work have Specificity? Authenticity? Variety? Intensity? Are your changes well-coordinated with the dings? Make a note in your practice journal, then keep working to improve.

Summary

I hope by now that I've convinced you that learning to work phrase by phrase is one of the most important things you can do to improve your singing acting. By clarifying the difference between working "moment to moment" and "phrase by phrase," I've shown why those two approaches are not incompatible with one another. I've shown how every phrase has a beginning, middle and end, and what you need to know about those 3 parts to execute each one successfully.

I'm also glad to have had the chance to introduce you to the "ding," one of the most significant concepts of SAVI singing acting. Dinging while singing will be a major key to your success on the musical stage. Once you've mastered the exercises in this chapter, you'll be ready to use this SAVI superpower to tackle the most complicated songs in the musical theater repertoire!

CHAPTER 7

What is Behavior?

An ounce of behavior is worth a pound of words.

—Sanford Meisner

Axiom 1, the primary principle of the SAVI System, tells you that your job as a singing actor is to "create behavior." So, let's dig more deeply into the notion of behavior: the types of behavior, how behavior communicates thoughts and feelings, and what you can do in class or in the studio to enhance your ability to create it.

The term **behavior** describes the various ways a person responds to a particular stimulus or situation. Stimuli can be internal or external, conscious or subconscious, and the person's response to it either voluntary or involuntary. In the following chapters, we'll explore the three main categories of behavior:

- Facial behavior, including facial expressions and eye movement;
- Vocal behavior, the ways your sound can change depending on what you're expressing or responding to;
- Physical behavior, including gestures and body language, as well as movement from one place to another.

How do we learn to create behavior? Much of our behavior is innate and instinctual. If we hurt ourselves, we don't need to be taught to cry out, and no one has to be taught to laugh when they are tickled. Many other behaviors, however, are learned; we learn to create (and, equally important, to suppress) behavior by imitating what we see in the world around us. We learn behavior like a language, and quickly come to understand what it means when someone winks or speaks with a growling tone or brandishes their middle finger. Gestures and behaviors can have different meanings in different cultures, and cultural norms will determine whether behavior is appropriate, excessive, or even offensive.

Behavior makes what is happening inside of you apparent on the outside. No one can see your thoughts or feelings, but your behavior provides tangible evidence of your otherwise intangible inner life. Your ability to express yourself behaviorally contributes to the quality commonly referred to as "stage presence," and you can cultivate both stage presence and behavioral expressiveness through deliberate practice.

Projective Modes of Behavior

There are three distinct ways in which the behavior of the singing actor is evident to audiences: the **voice, face,** and **body.** These are sometimes referred to as the three *projective modes*, and each of these independent channels is capable of conveying information to the audience in a manner that can either complement or contradicts the other two.

Every actor has a distinctive set of strengths and weaknesses when it comes to creating behavior. This is the result of our physical, psychological, temperamental and cultural differences, as well as our differences in training and experience. When you train for the musical stage, you must develop an extensive vocabulary of vocal, facial and physical behaviors, and learn to minimize unwanted entanglements or interference among them.

The term **vocal behavior** is an invitation to consider the idea of vocal expression more comprehensively. When you sing onstage, your voice must be capable of conveying a wide range of emotions, characterizations, and styles through choices of breath, support, placement, resonance, timbre and diction. Many singers and singing actors consider classical "bel canto" technique a valuable foundation, especially for roles written to feature the power, range, beauty and agility of the so-called "legit" voice. Labeling one style of singing as "legitimate," however, has the potential to reinforce an old-fashioned mindset in which non-classical styles are seen as somehow less "legitimate," less worthy and perhaps even dangerous. Modern-day singing-acting requires an open-minded, inclusive approach to vocal behavior, with access to a wide range of "unusual but useful" vocal sounds.

The types of behavior associated with vocal production can be usefully grouped into several subcategories that include breath choices, vowel resonance, diction choices, non-verbal vocal behaviors and musical choices. Breath involves the coordination of voice and body, while diction involves the coordination of voice and face (the muscles of articulation). Non-verbal behaviors include all sorts of sighs, grunts, laughs, growls and cries that convey meaning and emotion. Musical behaviors such as dynamics, articulation, and phrasing are sometimes included in the composer's notation, but are often created by the performer working in collaboration with a conductor, coach, and/or accompanist.

Facial behavior can be a touchy subject in performance training. We all know from personal experience that the face and eyes convey vast amounts of information about feelings and thoughts when we sing or speak, and even when we are silent. Opinions vary, however, about when the conscious use of the face and eyes devolves into "mugging," a pejorative term that refers to making silly, exaggerated faces. The idea that you might need to *deliberately* create facial behavior seems to run contrary to some acting teachers' notions of truth and authenticity. My experience, however, is that you'll need access to a wide range of expressive behaviors in both the face and the eyes to be an effective singing actor. There are ways to stretch, strengthen and activate those muscles so that your face will optimally express your inner thoughts and feelings without mugging.

Body behavior includes gesture, posture and body language as well as movement through space. As with the other two projective modes, your goal should be the development of an extensive vocabulary of behaviors, ranging from the most "natural" to the most "stylized." You should also cultivate the ability to change quickly and easily from one behavior to another as the dramatic moment dictates and to maintain a strong link between movement and the emotional life it expresses.

EXERCISE: Analyzing Behavior in YouTube Videos

Want a vivid illustration of the concept of behavior? Pick any song and watch three different performances of that song on YouTube. (Having begun my teaching career in the pre-Internet era, I have found YouTube to be a game-changer when it comes to studying the art of singing-acting.) In each video, the song is the same, so what's different? You might ask yourself:

- What different facial expressions does the singer use?
- When is there evidence of expressiveness in the eyes, or "eye language"?
- What kind of gestures does the singer use? What evidence of "body language" do I see?
- When does the singer alter or adjust their stance or location?
- What kind of vocal colors does the singer add? How do they breathe? Do they enunciate particular words or phrases in a way that adds meaning?
- What musical choices (tempo, dynamics, key) are evident in the performance?
- Are there any particular moments where a change in behavior seems particularly conspicuous?

Try this with your eyes closed (to focus on your sense of hearing) or with the sound off (to focus on what you see), and see if what you notice changes. As you take in the continuous "stream" of information that the performer uses to communicate, try to look for individual details (a shrug, a gesture, a flash of the eyes or a growl in the voice) that have particular impact. Notice how the singer's choices correlate to specific phrases and moments in the song.

Or do they? Maybe the video you're watching features behavior that's general, meaning that it's pretty much the same at every moment in the song. How effective are the performer's behavioral choices? Check the comments that have been posted and see what others think. They may corroborate your findings or give you reason to reconsider your judgments.

As you itemize and analyze the choices made by different performers singing the same song, you'll quickly discover the extent of each performer's creative contribution, and discern the opportunities for creative choice-making that any song presents. Your job as a singing actor is not to imitate YouTube's latest darling but to create your own unique performance. A song is a map that suggests a number of possible routes, and deciding which path you to take on your "journey of the song" will require energy and ingenuity.

"Psycho-Physicality" and Behavior

How much of the behavior you saw in the videos you analyzed do you think was spontaneous? How much was predetermined or "set?" How much was the sole creation of the performer, and how much was shaped or determined by a director, choreographer, or coach? It's hard to tell, of course, because when behavior is properly executed, it all seems to be a natural expression of the moment.

At any given moment in a singing actor's performance, behavior can be either externally or internally determined. ***Externally determined behavior*** is behavior that is "set" in advance; it can take the form of blocking, choreography, business,[20] or other behavior set by the director, choreographer, or conductor, or

[20] "Business" is a theatrical term that refers to the handling of props and other incidental onstage activity that doesn't fit into the categories of blocking or choreography. My graduate directing teacher, Larry Carra, had an elegant name for it in his book *Fundamentals of Stage Directing*: he called it "pantomimic dramatization." Now *there's* a fancy bit of MFA jargon.

behavior that the actor himself has chosen and planned prior to the performance. In contrast, **internally determined behavior** is unplanned, occurring in reaction to some stimulus or change in the world of the play or thanks to an intuitive process on the part of the actor. If you detect some overlap between externally and internally determined behavior, go to the head of the class! The choices you discover spontaneously during the rehearsal process usually get "set," with the expectation that you'll repeat them consistently over multiple performances.

Making choices in the theater is a complicated business. Acting is an intensely collaborative art form, which means the rehearsal room and the stage are full of loud, bossy people with lots of opinions. The writers (whether present or absent, living or dead) have set down a fairly specific notion of the dramatic event through the particular words, notes and phrases they have chosen. The conductor, the director, the choreographer and an army of assistants and other ancillary personnel are also bursting with ideas about what your choices should be.

But that shouldn't mean you don't get some say in the matter. In the moment of performance, it's your ass up there (as one might say in the colorful parlance of showbiz), not the writer's or the conductor's or any else's, and that means the choosing must include you as well. When you sing, you must always be choosing, and the foundation for determining the most interesting, creative, useful choices is a rock-solid understanding of the dramatic event: What's happening now? Who's doing what to whom, and why is it important?

What comes first, the behavior or the thought or feeling it expresses? It's a chicken-and-egg dilemma that Stanislavski resolves by formulating a notion he calls "psycho-physicality," a way of thinking about behavior as both internal and external, a manifestation of an inner state as well as a means of entering into that state. Years of experience have validated my belief in a "psycho-physical" approach to singing-acting, one that recognizes that choices can legitimately originate either in the inner life or on the outer surface, as long as the connection between those two worlds is scrupulously honored and maintained. The distinction between "inside-out" and "outside-in" that's been argued by generations of actors and their teachers is, in my view, a false duality: the relationship between your inner state and the external behavior by which it is manifested is *duplex*, a two-way street.

Creating behavior and organizing it into a performance means making changes sometimes, but at other times, it means *not* making changes. The singing actor must know when to make a change in his behavior and when to sustain behavior without changing. Doing too much in between dings can muddy the water, confuse your spectator and distract from your otherwise good work. When you're in between dings, keep it simple and focus on sustaining, maintaining and developing your choices.

Mastering both choosing and changing will give you the ability to create work that is articulate and intelligently structured. Choosing without changing results in static, one-dimensional behavior, while changing without choosing results in random, chaotic behavior that is equally unsatisfactory. Study the script, the score, the given circumstances and the behavior of your onstage partners for clues about when to sustain a choice and when to make a change.

Why is Behavior Often Absent from a Performance?

The absence of behavior, in life or onstage, can create a sense of mystery or of information withheld, but more frequently it is interpreted as lifelessness, a "woodenness" more suited to statues than to humans who aspire to believable expression.

Why is behavior so often absent from the performances of singing actors? Why is it that so many singers exhibit behavior that conveys the general effort of singing rather than the specific behavior of a real person living truthfully under imaginary circumstances?

Well, first and foremost, fear and its insidious companion, tension, are to blame. When we are afraid, we suppress our impulses for fear of being (or appearing to be) wrong. Timidity and shyness are usually byproducts of fear.

Second, lack of behavior may come from the ineffective management of the effort of singing. Great singing is indeed hard work, especially when it comes to vocal extremes (high notes, loud notes, long notes), but part of the art of singing is expressing oneself with ease, even when the work is challenging.

Finally, lack of behavior may come from lack of adequate preparation. This may mean that you have failed to explore the possibilities thoughtfully or to rehearse sufficiently to ensure that your behavior is expressive and truthful even under the stressful circumstances of performance.

Happily, all three of these problems can be addressed through training. Having embraced Axiom 1 of the SAVI System, the singing actor clearly understands the work he or she is undertaking: "When I sing, I will create behavior that communicates the dramatic event phrase by phrase."

With all that in mind, let's turn our attention to some of the most valuable exercises in the SAVI System, ones designed to help you practice creating behavior while singing. Fasten your seat-belts, kids; I've got quite a few of them!

EXERCISE: Lip Sync

"Lip sync" is short for "lip synchronization," a kind of mimed performance synchronized to a recording in which you invent silent behavior to create the illusion you are actually singing the song. But then you knew that already, didn't you? Not only that, but you probably don't need me to explain that lip-syncing involves more than just your lips, right? Just checking.

I had a personal experience with lip-syncing in one of my rare forays into the world of professional performance, when I appeared in the *Sweeney Todd* scene of Kevin Smith's 2004 film *Jersey Girl*. The music track for that scene, including all the vocals, was pre-recorded and then played back during the shoot. While filming, the cast sang along with the track, and knowing that my vocal performance was already "in the can," I felt wonderfully free to craft the physical and facial components of my performance without having to fret about my singing.

It is fascinating to see how non-singing behaviors (facial expression, eye language, body movement, and gesture) blossom once the singer is liberated from the fear and tension that so often accompany the effort to sing well. The new ideas you discover through the lip-sync process can then be integrated into your singing performance.

Lip-syncing is great to do on your own or in a classroom setting. The procedures described below are easily adapted for a group class. In a group setting, I find that students are inspired and excited by one another's work and that the discussions that follow are invariably productive.

Level 1. Pick a recording of a song and "lip-sync" it–that is, devise a performance intended to create the illusion that you are actually singing the song. It doesn't have to be a musical theater song, or even a song sung by someone of the same gender as you! Lip-syncing different sorts of songs invites you to explore new and unfamiliar sorts of behavior. Take advantage of the temporary freedom that lip-syncing affords you; without the demands of actually having to sing, you can devote your full attention and creativity to the challenge of generating behavior in the face, eyes and body. This can be a remarkably productive means of exploring the behavioral possibilities of a song you intend to perform. Use a video camera to record yourself, and play back your performance. Does your work seem freer, more inventive and expressive in the lip-synched version? Make a note of the discoveries you'd like to incorporate when you sing.

Level 2. Make an audio recording of yourself singing a piece that you are working on, and use it as the soundtrack for a lip-synced performance. Make a video recording of yourself lip-syncing to your pre-recorded voice, and then one where you actually sing the song. Examine the videos and see what this tells you about the creation of behavior and its role in the communication of the song. Use the lip-sync recording to discover new choices to incorporate into your sung performance.

EXERCISE: Gibberish

Gibberish is one of my favorite tools for exploring and strengthening your ability to create behavior. The word "gibberish" means "nonsense" or "meaningless noise," but when you use gibberish as a performance training tool, your sounds will become full of meaning. Gibberish is communication without intelligible language, which forces you to use behavior to express yourself. Use the following activities to work on your gibberish skills.

1. **Spoken Gibberish with SAVI Cards.** Choose a SAVI Card to serve as a catalyst for your improvised gibberish. Start out with action verbs, such as "to plead" or "to explain," and adjectives ("calm," "urgent") and use these catalysts to inform and inspire your exploration of gibberish sounds. Try combining verbs and adjectives (How is "to plead" + "calm" different from "to plead" + "urgent?").

Next, try a Face Card as a catalyst. Make your face look like the picture on the card, and see what gibberish sounds come out when you "inhabit" that face. Or imagine yourself speaking to the person whose face is pictured on the card. Make a sequence of several cards, and explore what happens as you transition from one card to the next. This simulates the phrase-by-phrase approach you use when singing a song.

2. **Sung Gibberish with SAVI Cards.** All of the activities in Step 1 can be sung, using either freely improvised music or phrases or patterns from songs or vocal exercises you know. When you're ready, use music catalyst cards ("louder," "higher," "more beautiful") to deliberately shape your musical choices. If you're working alone in the practice room, you'll be singing *a cappella*, but with a little bit of luck, you'll hook up with an accompanist or coach who's willing to jam with you.

When you start to sing gibberish, does it feel different? Explore moving back and forth between spoken and sung gibberish. In what ways do they feel different? Can you remain as behaviorally free when you sing as you are when you speak?

3. **Gibberish Soliloquy (Spoken or Sung)**. Take a song or aria you're working on, and use its dramatic event and imaginary circumstances as the basis for an improvised soliloquy (either spoken or sung). Record your work on video and study the behavior you created. Incorporate those ideas into your performance of that song.

4. **Gibberish Translation.** Work on a piece of repertoire you are singing, but substitute gibberish sounds for the words of the song. Record on video, and compare what's different when you sing the regular words versus the gibberish sounds.

Working in the classroom or with a group expands the number of possible gibberish activities you can use to strengthen your ability to create behavior.

1. Gibberish Call-and-Response. Working in a circle, speak or sing a gibberish phrase, then have the group echo that phrase. Give SAVI Cards to your fellow students to provoke ideas about the content or quality of the phrase.

2. Gibberish Conversation (Spoken). Pick another student, and improvise a conversation in a made-up language. Decide on a set of imaginary circumstances to establish a dramatic event for your conversation.

3. Gibberish Arias and Duets (Sung). Improvised singing frightens many singing actors, who feel much more comfortable executing a pre-existing score than they do making stuff up. If you fall into that category, let me reassure you that it's not only productive but fun as well! My experience is that working with gibberish and improvised singing quickly becomes a playful, joyful experience. This activity can be done with or without accompaniment (of course, it helps to have an intrepid, creative pianist), and can also incorporate a conductor, SAVI Cards, or gesture shopping

(p. 165). This is a great way to generate new musical material in a collaboratively creative, devised-theater setting!

EXERCISE: Speak and Sing

I've observed that singers treat language very differently when they speak and when they sing. For this reason, I recommend making time in your conditioning session to work on exploring what happens when you speak and sing the same text. Here's a good procedure to use:

- Choose a SAVI Phrase Card from the deck. Take a moment to imagine a dramatic circumstance under which you might speak that phrase. Use the Fundamental Questions to guide you in developing that dramatic circumstance (see below, p. 188?)
- Speak the text on your card aloud. Repeat it, trying some different line readings. Add behavior, using the face and body as well as the voice, until you feel like you're communicating the drama of the text in a way that is both Specific and Authentic.
- As you continue to repeat the text, elongate its vowel sounds and start to "nudge" your line reading in the direction of a sung sound. See if you can make more specific choices about pitch and melody as you craft a tune for the text you're speaking.
- Notice what happens as you move from speaking to singing. Can you keep the same feeling of Specificity and Authenticity you had when you were speaking? Once you've found a "melody" in your line reading, try shifting the pitch of the whole melody up or down on subsequent repetitions.
- As an option, use other SAVI Cards (one at a time) to modify your behavioral choices when you speak and sing the phrase.
- If you're working on a piece of text from a song, sing it out fully, with your best voice-lesson voice, then

start to modify your sound to make it slightly more speechlike with each repetition until you're not singing at all.

Study the results of this experiment by video-recording yourself and comparing what happens when you sing with what happens when you speak. Do any of the changes you make when you sing affect your other behavioral modes (face, eyes, body language) in a way that diminishes your believability? Repeat this experiment, practicing over and over and treating the "middle ground" between a fully spoken text and a fully sung text as a spectrum of possibilities to be explored.

EXERCISE: Content-Neutral Songs

Songs that don't have specific meaning or dramatic content are good for working on the technical aspects of singing-acting, especially your ability to make adjustments in your behavior in coordination with the dings.

"The Five-Note Phrase" is a simple étude that can help you practice the skill of choosing and changing behavior over the course of a song. Use SAVI Cards to prompt you to make a wide range of choices, including in the realms of tone, timbre, gesture and facial expression. As you do, you'll also develop your ability to transition effectively between choices in coordination with the musical score. Sheet music for accompaniment to "The Five-Note Phrase" can be found in this book's Additional Resources section, along with information about recorded karaoke versions available on www.SAVISingingActor.com. If an accompanist or a recorded version is not available for your current practice session, please note that the étude works well as an *a cappella* exercise, too. In fact, it can be done at different tempos and with different styles of vocal production.

This version of the music, in a six-four time signature, is a good place to start when you're new to this exercise. The melody, as you can see, is based on an ascending and descending major scale. The printed lyric is just one of several options you can use to sing it. It's also quite useful to use solfège syllables (do-re-mi and so on) when you sing this etude. The mental effort of recalling the proper syllables and singing them in the correct order may tie your brain in knots, but it's a great workout for using multiple regions of the brain simultaneously.

The music is marked with ding symbols(Δ) at the end of every two measures. These dings are placed based on the meaning of the words in the lyric I've provided, but if you're singing vowel sounds or solfège syllables, you can place the dings on the last beat of any or every measure, as you prefer. In a group class, the teacher or a designated assistant can make a sound (using a desk bell, tone bar or triangle, or even saying "ding!") where the dings occur. If you're working alone, try making a sound like a hand clap, finger snap or thigh slap at each ding to give yourself a disruptive signal at the moments where change occurs. Remember, each ding is a moment to breathe in as you make the transition to a new phrase, a new idea and a new choice.

Once you've got the hang of singing and dinging this particular étude, throw some behavioral choices into the mix. Choose a few SAVI Cards from the same category (two Action Cards, for instance), and sing the song while making behavioral choices, switching from one card to the next at each ding. You can either hold the cards in your hand while you sing, or lay them all out on a music stand or flat surface so that you can see your next choice at a glance without having to involve your hands. As in all SAVI Card exercises, make an effort to truly *inhabit* the behavior you create. In other words, try to find an organic link between your external behavior and your emotional and dramatic inner life.

Depending on the key you start with and the number of times you **modulate** (raising the key in half-steps), you can cover a substantial vocal range in this exercise. You'll be surprised by the amount of vocal energy the exercise releases, and you should remind yourself to breathe and support your singing, since you may otherwise find yourself yelling without meaning to.

The six-four version of the étude gives you an opportunity to sustain the final note of each phrase for a few beats and not feel rushed by the arrival of the "ding." Try out different cards, different keys and different tempos in order to calmly and methodically "settle in" to the pattern of choosing and changing. When you're ready, try introducing more cards. You can use as many as eight if you're not using the printed lyric.

A Five Note Phrase (solo version)

SAVI System etude

Charles Gilbert

This version of the music has four beats in each bar. It leaves you with less time to sustain the fifth note in each phrase and instead forces you to hurry along your transition to the next phrase, which should feel slightly more challenging. (If you're feeling clever, you can adjust the music and sing it in 3/4 or even 5/8 meter for an even greater challenge!)

EXERCISE: The Mirror Canon

You'll get enormous benefits from working on the Five-Note Phrase étude on your own. When it's done with a partner, though, it takes your learning to a whole new level by introducing elements of interpersonal communication and behavioral give-and-take. In this section, I explain how to adapt the Five-Note Phrase into a group exercise called the Mirror Canon.

Stand facing your partner and decide who'll sing first (the Leader) and who'll sing second (the Follower). If there are more than two of you in the rehearsal space, I recommend organizing the group into two lines facing one another, with the Leaders on one side and the Followers on the other. With an odd number of participants, have one student stand apart and observe the exercise.

Once you've mastered the music of the exercise, the Leaders will add behavior to each phrase of the canon, and the Followers will "mirror" that behavior when it's their turn to sing. When the verse is complete, the music modulates up a half-step and the Follower(s) now become the Leader(s). After a few repetitions, it is often useful to have a student from the end of one line move to the other end of the line, so that each student in that line will shift to a new partner on the opposite line.

As with the solo version of this exercise, the canon is first presented in a version that has six beats to each bar (a 6/4 time signature). It may take a few tries for the students to keep their "dings" appropriately synchronized with their respective vocal lines. Initially, the music should be sung and played at a moderate tempo, though eventually the tempo and style can vary. When you're ready, you can also introduce the 4/4 version of the exercise (again, see sheet music in the appendix).

First "Mirror Canon" Variation: Vowel Sounds

Have the Leader randomly choose a different vowel sound for each five-note phrase, and the Follower copy those vowel sounds. Once the music has completed, switch roles and repeat. The 12 options for vowel sounds are the ones featured in the "Aught of Art" song introduced in the Chapter 5 voice warm-up and reprised in Chapter 9.

Second "Mirror Canon" Variation: Facial Expression

The Leader randomly chooses a different facial expression to accompany each vowel sound, and the Follower mimics or mirrors those faces. This can be done mechanically (i.e., facial gymnastics), but it's better to "inhabit" each facial expression—that is, to create an inner state that in some way matches or supports what the face is doing. Again, once the music has completed, switch roles and repeat.

As you begin to activate your face while singing, your first impulse may be to thrust your face toward your partner, which results in an uncomfortable, unhealthy, and unflattering forward translation of the head beyond its balance point at the top of the spine. Try to allow your head to remain balanced atop the spine even when your face is highly energized. Explore all your facial muscles in this exercise: the forehead, the eyebrows, the muscles around the eyes, the cheeks, the lips, the nose, the jaw, and so on. Use different sectors of the face alone and in combination. Explore both big and small choices, "truthful" and "phony" choices, beautiful and ugly choices. Using dialectical pairs of qualities like these can help you explore a full range of possibilities. You may notice your changing facial expressions produce a corresponding change in your sounds. That's a good thing!

Third "Mirror Canon" Variation: Body Language

The Leader makes a physical choice-a gesture or statement in body language-to accompany each phrase, and the Follower mimics each choice. This can (and should) be done both separately from the face and together with the face.

If you're a teacher leading this exercise from the sidelines, here are some common issues you should watch out for and ways you can coach your students productively:

(1) As with the previous round, you must commit strongly to your choices and inhabit each one fully. This is a psycho-physical exercise, and the participants should be invited to explore the reciprocal "duplex" relationship that exists between outward behavior and inner emotional life.

(2) Encouragement participants to use a wide variety of choices. Are there certain choices they "default" to? Would some SAVI Cards help you mix things up? The cards can be introduced as catalysts in any variation of the exercise.

(3) The Follower can be instructed to exaggerate the Leader's behavior, much like a magnifying mirror or something you'd find in a carnival funhouse.

If it hasn't come up already, encourage the student participants to create one, and only one, choice per phrase. This will reinforce the habit of committing strongly and impulsively to a choice at the beginning of each phrase, and then sustaining and inhabiting that choice for the duration of the musical phrase. If the participants in this exercise are constantly in motion, then they're not doing it right; there should be a swift and strong initiation of behavior at the beginning of the phrase, after which the choice should be efficiently sustained—with only the amount of effort needed, no excess tension—for the duration of the phrase. The singer need not "freeze" in each pose, but should not introduce any new choices in the middle of a phrase either.

Fourth "Mirror Canon" Variation: Imitation and Interaction

While maintaining the musical score of the exercise, begin to explore what happens when the Follower chooses behavior that is not a mirror or imitation of the "Leader, but rather an impulsive response to the Leader's choice.

In this case, the exercise begins to acquire more of the give-and-take quality of a conversation, at least at the behavioral level. For instance, in the first five-note phrase, the Leader might create vocal and physical behavior that is harsh and aggressive; in response, the Follower might be intimidated by that behavior and respond meekly and submissively. The Leader, in turn, might respond to the Follower's meekness with a new choice, creating behavior that is apologetic. Explore what happens when imitative choices and interactive choices become mingled. Say to your fellow participants, "You have the choice of either imitating your partner or responding impulsively with a different choice that is a reaction to their choice." You can also present them with a structured sequence, such as four imitations followed by four interactions, or pairs of imitations and interactions.

Fifth "Mirror Canon" Variation: Structure

There are many cases in which singing actors are called upon to execute pre-planned behavior choices along with spontaneous choices in a way that seems authentic. This variation makes it possible to explore that challenge in the creative context of an exercise. Use SAVI Cards for the pre-planned choices if that feels useful to your group.

Have the Leaders decide on two specific gesture/face/voice combinations. Have them practice these both individually and in alternation. In the exercise, have them use Combination #1 on the first and third phrases and Combination #2 on the second and fourth phrases . Each time Combination #1 or #2 occurs, side-coach the participants to ensure that it is as specific and truthful as possible, and to maximize the contrast between the two combinations.

As a variation, have the Leaders decide on one specific gesture/face/voice combination, and use it in alternation with a random selection of other choices. In other words, they will follow the pattern of Combination #1 (first phrase)/Random choice (second phrase)/Combination #1 (third phrase)/Another random choice (fourth phrase), and so on.

Sixth "Mirror Canon" Variation: Choices from Repertoire

Many days you will come to class with prepared repertoire to present. Warm up using the Mirror Canon to choose sounds, facial expressions, and physical choices like the ones you will use in the song you're going to present.

I've had great results with all of the variations of the Mirror Canon when I use them as part of the warm-up or as conditioning work in my class. Initially, you may find it exciting because of its novelty, but it's important to treat this not as a quirky one-and-done experience, but as an exercise to be done repeatedly. Just like calisthenics, yoga asanas or work at the ballet barre, the Mirror Canon is an exercise that requires discipline, attention to correct form, and mindfulness of its goals. These goals are:

- To acquire the habit of creating expressive behavior while singing;
- To acquire the habit of making choices, inhabiting those choices, and then making new and different choices in coordination with a musical event;

- To expand your "behavioral vocabulary"–that is, the range of choices you can confidently and truthfully inhabit and employ in performance;
- To acquire good habits of use while singing and acting, including maintaining a balanced position of the head atop the spine while creating strong facial, physical and emotional choices, learning to initiate a variety of new choices impulsively without inhibitory tension, and learning to sustain choices for the duration of a phrase without excessive effort.

Behavior When You're NOT Singing

Meisner's axiom, "An ounce of behavior is worth a pound of words," is especially relevant in moment of silence. This includes those times when no one on stage is speaking, and also when someone else is speaking and your job as an actor is to remain present in the scene with no lines to speak or sing.

The first heartbeat. One of the most important moments in which you must create behavior is the instrumental introduction to a song, when you're preparing to sing your first words. Make it your habit to create behavior to fill this "first heartbeat" based both on your relationship with your partner and your understanding of the imaginary circumstances at the moment the song starts. To help you clarify your choices, you can write a line or two of inner monologue to say to yourself during the first heartbeat, and then use that to prompt your behavioral choices.

It is helpful to think about "stirring the soup" during the introduction to a song or, for that matter, whenever a significant transitional moment such as an interlude occurs in your song. When you "stir the soup," you deliberately disrupt whatever your previous state was by initiating some new behavior. The behavior itself can be fairly insignificant: a bit of facial flex, moving the muscles of the eyes to look around, changing your stance or focus. It's helpful to introduce new behavioral energy into a song at critical moments, like a cook might use a spoon to get the bits that may have settled to the bottom of the pan suspended in a soup's broth again. Sometimes all it takes is the simplest of choices to break the "logjam" of inertia and bring the song back to life.

Creating behavior when it's not your turn to sing. When you sing a duet, do you "check out" and stop acting when you're not singing? This is one of the most common mistakes I see singing actors make. I'm going to go out on a limb and say that what you do when you're *not* singing is every bit as important as what you do when you *are*. In this regard, Axiom 1 gets it a little bit wrong; to be completely accurate, it should read, "When you sing **and even when you're not singing**, your job is to create behavior that communicates the dramatic event phrase by phrase."

It is especially important when you're singing alone on the stage, soliloquy-style, that your moments of silence include "an ounce of behavior." What you do during the introduction, the interludes, the transitional moments and the moments of listening to a real or imaginary partner are crucial to achieving specificity, authenticity and variety in your performance. When you get hyper-focused on your vocal delivery, as some soloists do, you can lose sight of the fact that what you do when you're not singing is every bit as important to the act of communication. There's more to say on this topic in Chapter 11, when we talk about Input and Output.

EXERCISE: Active Listening

In the practice room, put on a recording of a song or a speech, and imagine you're the one being sung or spoken to. (Of course, you can do this in the classroom with a live partner, but doing this in the practice room can also help you get the hang of it.) As the actor in the recording comes to the end of each phrase, make yourself say out loud the last few words of the phrase you just heard, or the two or three words that seemed most important to you. If you need to, change the pronouns from first person to second person ("I" to "you") or the other way around. Then add a few words of your own to make your point of view about what you've just heard clear.

This exercise is designed to help you build the important habits of:

- actively listening for the content of the phrase being sung;
- deciding on a point of view about what's being sung and how it's been sung;
- and then expressing that point of view in the words you choose to repeat and the behavior that accompanies those words.

Having practiced verbalizing your responses, now play the recording again. This time, don't say your responses out loud, just say them in your head instead. Make sure your point of view and your behavior are just as clear as before; just don't speak out loud. "Inner monologue" is the technical term that describes what you're doing. You're taking the flow of thoughts and feelings that goes through your head and trying to make it specific and concrete by choosing particular external behaviors to embody and express it.

When you do this with a recording, you'll be speaking over the recording, and the recorded performance will continue regardless of what you say or how you say it. If you do this as an exercise with a live singing partner, your interjections will interrupt the flow of the song, which may or may not be useful. We'll explore this option more fully in Part V, when we discuss partner work and its role in achieving Maximum Authenticity.

Summary

This chapter was intended to be a comprehensive exploration of the concept of behavior, and as with previous chapters, we've covered a lot of ground. I introduced three principal types of projective behavior, the three "channels" we use to "broadcast" our thoughts and feelings: face (including eyes), voice and body. Each of these will get carefully examined in the next three chapters.

We discussed ways you can examine the behavior of other singing actors on video, a skill that will come in handy when it comes time to assess your own work via video playback. I introduced the concept of "psycho-physicality," another way of approaching the duplex relationship of outer behavior and inner life. And I presented you with a number of exercises you can use to practice creating behavior while singing and coordinating it with a musical score: the number-one skill every singing actor needs to master! Now, off to the practice room!

CHAPTER 8

Your Face is Your Ace!

Stand in front of a mirror and you'll find yourself face to face with your most powerful "organ of expression." The 40 or so different muscles underneath the skin of your face are capable of creating thousands of different facial expressions whose chief purpose seems to be transmitting information to those around you. Your face might say, "I'm friendly, please approach!" It might say, "I'm confused, can you help me?" or even, "I'm in the mood for love, are you?" Your facial expressions communicate emotions instantaneously and powerfully, often without any conscious effort or intent on your part.

To realize your full potential as a singing actor, you need to learn to "play your ace," the most valuable card you've got, by learning to use your face and your eye movements to their full advantage. For a start, this means exercising and toning your facial muscles so that they become more flexible and more responsive to your expressive impulses. It means exploring the ways in which those muscles are used to produce expression, expanding your "vocabulary" of facial expressions. And it means learning how to counteract the facial distortions that sometimes occur while singing to make sure your face is conveying more than simply the effort of singing.

Tone of voice, facial expression, and eye and body language account for a much greater percentage of the information you communicate than your words do. How much more? One study found that only 7% of what you communicate is the result of the actual words you use, while the other 93% can be attributed to body language and tone of voice.[21] If the words you're saying aren't congruent with your behavior, people are likely to disregard your words and heed your non-verbal messages instead. In the world of singing-acting, facial incongruity is a very familiar phenomenon. For example, imagine someone singing the words "I love you" using high pitches and a loud voice. Chances are the expression on their face is going to be tense and straining rather than tender and inviting. Which do you think you'd be more likely to believe: the words or the face?

The face and its role in the expression of emotions have been the subject of considerable study over the past two centuries. More recently, scientists like Silvan Tomkins and psychologist Paul Ekman have made considerable advances in our understanding of the face. Ekman pioneered the term "micro-expressions" to describe the small, fleeting facial movements that can reveal our true, inner thoughts. Ekman's work was the basis for the television show *Lie to Me*, where a scientist (loosely based on Ekman) taught criminal investigators and detectives how to interpret micro-expressions to discern lies from truth.[22]

Early researchers proposed the idea that facial expressions, once thought to be just the visible sign of an emotion, can be used deliberately to bring on a feeling. In fact, Paul Ekman has demonstrated that the conscious use of certain facial muscles can arouse organic emotional responses. For example, if you smile, your mood will begin to lift. The Chilean pedagogue Susana Bloch has made an intensive study of how emotions manifest themselves in the face, breath and body, and teaches actors to use those "effector patterns" to induce (and neutralize) those emotional states. The technique she calls Alba Emoting™ is an innovative "psycho-physical" approach that helps actors create and control emotion.

---

[21] This statistic comes from the research of Dr. Paul Mehrabian at UCLA, author of *Nonverbal Communcation* (New York: Routledge, 2017).
[22] "Lie to Me," *Paul Ekman Group*, www.paulekman.com/projects/lie-to-me/.

In his books *The Complete Singer-Actor, Performing Power,* and *The Radiant Performer,* author Wesley Balk proposes that expressive communication takes place in three areas: the voice, body, and face. His analysis of the face and its role in the expression of emotion while singing remains seminal and enormously important. In his research, Balk noticed that students with a background in singing were more open to exploring the technical aspects of facial communication than those with a background in acting: "The idea of making faces, grimacing to convey emotions, or even working with facially oriented techniques is anathema to those who have studied and worked in American theater traditions.... Actors were more resistant than singers because [of these] ... preconceived notions.... Singers, being involved in a highly technical act to begin with, accepted the concept more readily.... [T]he change and growth made available through the exercise and development of the facial/emotional mode have been genuinely astonishing."[23]

Do you hesitate to "use your face" when you act? Perhaps you've heard warnings from your acting teachers about the dangers of mugging. To acting teacher Sanford Meisner, trying to manufacture emotion or counterfeit its expression on the face was one of the biggest mistakes an actor can make. "Leave yourself alone!" is an aphoristic bit of advice frequently heard in a Meisner class, but my experience is that when you leave your face alone while singing, you may wind up expressing very little apart from the effort of singing, even if you're in a strong state of emotional arousal. These facial distortions are further compounded by the natural tendency many of us have to *conceal* rather than *reveal* our innermost feelings.

Finding a comfortable middle ground between phony, cheesy mugging and the tense, blank mask of the straining singer is a goal that is well worth pursuing. If you follow the steps described in the exercises below, you'll begin to develop your

---

[23] H. Wesley Balk, *Performing Power* (Minneapolis: University of Minnesota Press, 1985), 141-2.

face into a more effective tool of expression and discover why "your face is your ace" in successful singing-acting.

Facial Flex: Activate the Muscles in Your Face

Exercising the muscles of your face will increase your ability to create effective facial expressions. It will also help keep the muscles of your face toned and vibrant, which has the secondary benefit of diminishing the effects of aging. A YouTube search will turn up lots of videos demonstrating "Facercise," "Face Yoga," "Facerobics" and "Face Gym," any of which will enhance your powers of facial expression as a performer by increasing the vitality and tone of your face.

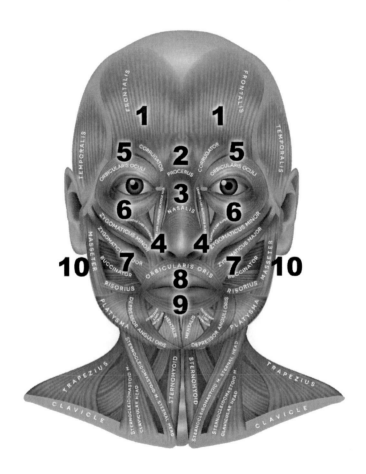

Try a systematic "facial flex" to stretch and energize every muscle in your face before singing or performing. As you look into the mirror, see if you can move each of the 10 zones identified on the figure above:

1. Forehead - contract and relax
2. Corrugator - squeeze eyebrows together to scowl, then relax
3. Nose - wriggle, lift and lower
4. Nostrils - flare and relax
5. Eyelid - lift up, close and press down
6. Muscles below the Eye - squint, wink
7. Muscles of the Cheeks - raise to a smile, then drop
8. The Upper Lip - rub over teeth, snarl, sneer
9. The Lower Lip - puff out to pout, pull in
10. Muscles That Control the Jaw - raise and lower jaw, move from side to side

Follow this up with some freestyle "gurning," in which you move the muscles in any and all of the 10 groups to make crazy faces and sounds. In a class, it's helpful to do this while standing opposite a partner and mirroring the other's face in alternating roles as leader and follower. The natural dynamic of imitation, cooperation and competition in this mirror exercise will take your work to new levels of specificity and intensity.

CAUTION: While you were making faces, did you notice a tendency to thrust your head forward? As discussed in Chapter 7, this distortion of alignment is a common occurrence when you increase the amount of energy you use in your face. If you're not sure, use a video camera or have your partner check the relationship among your head, neck and torso from a profile view while you're practicing a vigorous facial flex. You want to keep the head poised and balanced atop the spine and the neck free and easy regardless of how much activity you're generating with your facial muscles.

Making Faces and Facial "Masks": Choosing and Changing Facial Expressions

In SAVI Singing Acting, the job of the singing actor is to create behavior that communicates the dramatic event **phrase by phrase**. The concept of working "phrase by phrase" has important implications for how you use your face. This means being able to change or adjust your facial expression at the beginning of a phrase and then sustain and develop that choice for the duration of the phrase. For this reason, it's useful to practice making and sustaining "facial masks."

During the facial flex warm-up, you move the individual muscles of your face, but when you make a facial mask, you arrange those muscles to make a particular "picture" with your face. As with the facial flex, you can do this with a mirror, video camera, partner or group. Collect some photographs of faces in extremes of emotional expression (anger, fear, happiness, sadness, disgust, curiosity, tenderness, eroticism, and joy) for inspiration and practice those as "masks."

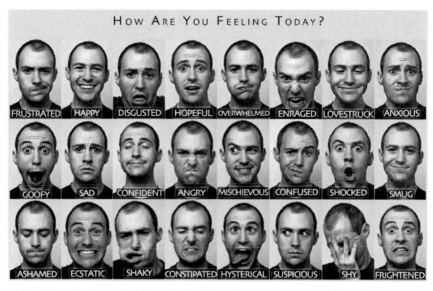

Here's a whole mini-gallery of facial masks to inspire you. I love this image from Facebook but couldn't determine who created these pictures. Look how he uses all the different zones and muscles of the face!

Practice "putting on the mask" all at once, then sustaining and intensifying its expression (without tension in the neck!) for 10-15 seconds. Then release that effort and allow the face to return to neutral or to change to a new mask.

CAUTION: While you were sustaining a mask, did you notice you had a tendency to stop breathing? Try to use your breath to support and animate what's happening on your face. If your facial expression shows anguish, find an anguished breath; if your face communicates bliss, let a blissful breath or sound move through that mask. Explore the sounds-non-verbal sounds, gibberish sounds, even sung sounds-that emanate from each unique combination of face, breath and imagination.

Get Inspired by Pictures of Faces

SAVI Cards are a great way to explore facial behavior and expand your vocabulary of expressions. The images in the cards are photos of actors, but you may find images in other sources that inspire you. If you see a picture in a magazine, book or gallery that intrigues you, snap a picture of it with your phone. Print your pictures and paste them onto SAVI Custom Cards or use a digital tool like Google Photos or Pinterest to organize your collection of pictures into albums or "boards" that you can access when you practice.

When you're working with a picture of a face, hold the card (or the screen of your phone) up to eye level. Imagine that you are looking into a hand mirror and arrange the muscles on your face to match the picture in front of you. If you're working alone, use a mirror or video camera to compare your facial expression with the picture on the card. Try to match every detail of the picture: the forehead, the eyebrows, the eyes, the nose, the cheeks, the lips and so on. Once you're satisfied that you've fully "put on" that mask, now try to inhabit it. Imagine what thoughts or feelings go with that face, and create some inner monologue to support those thoughts and feelings. How would someone making that kind of a face breathe?

After a few moments, you may want to go back and check the picture. See if you need to recommit to any of the details on your own face. Can you intensify your facial expression by one percent? By five? Or should you dial it down a notch or two? Explore different levels of intensity as you breathe through the mask and create an inner monologue to support your corresponding emotional state.

Try speaking or singing a word through the mask: "Yes!" "No!" "Why?" "Please!" Then, speak or sing some gibberish sounds through that facial mask. Next, sing a vocal phrase while inhabiting the mask. Try singing that phrase higher, lower, louder, softer, quicker or slower, but maintain the "mask" as you do this.

After 15 seconds or so, give your face a rest and try another card. I do this exercise in class with the participants standing in a circle. Each participant has a different card, and they pass their cards to one another when it's time to change. If you're working alone, simply choose the next card from your deck or your Pinterest board and repeat.

The SAVI Card set also includes some face "icons" that invite you to explore what happens when you deliberately activate different muscle groups while you sing. What happens when you activate your forehead and eyebrows? The muscles around your eyes? The muscles of the cheeks and nose? The muscles around your mouth?

After you've done some conditioning and exploratory play using the Face Cards, see if you can apply them to an étude or song, using a different "mask" for each phrase. Remember, it's most effective to change your facial expressions when a new phrase begins and leave it relatively unchanged for the duration of the phrase. It doesn't matter if the mask matches the emotions of the song exactly. Indeed, there's plenty of room for creative discovery by trying out faces that you might initially think "don't fit."

It may not be necessary to decide on the exact nature of the facial expression you're going to use next so long as you know you commit to making a change. Not only do the changes in your facial expression bring greater variety to your performance, but spectators will also ascribe meaning to those changes even when they're random or arbitrary. Use a video camera or partner for feedback, and you'll see what I mean.

CAUTION: Be on the lookout for distortions of the facial musculature during a song. Often, those distortions are simply an indication of the effort of singing, especially when the pitches are high or loud. Sometimes, a singer will try to "locate" the sensation of their sound in a particular part of the face to intensify a certain resonance, which can lead to facial distortions. Make a video recording of your face while you're singing, and a second recording of yourself speaking the text you sang. Do they look different? In what ways? If your face says, "I'm singing" or "I'm making a fine tone," chances are that's the only message your listeners are getting. Make sure you pay attention to what your face does during moments of extreme vocalism: Do your eyebrows shoot up on high notes? Do your mouth and lips make distorted, unnatural shapes for "pure" vowels? You should seek to develop both awareness and ease in your use of facial expression, using the tools of deliberate practice (i.e., specific goals and frequent prompt feedback) to guide your progress.

Eye Language

Your eyes play a particularly important role in facial communication and expression. An ancient proverb states that "the eyes are the window to the soul," and we've all seen how the subtlest movement of the eyes can convey deep emotion in film and TV acting. You might be surprised to realize just how much impact your eyes have in a live stage performance, too. As a singing actor, you must learn to "match your gaze to the phrase" and use your eyes to their fullest advantage.

Watch a video of a performance you think is particularly effective and make an inventory of the singer's behavior, paying special attention to the way they use their eyes. Do you see how the singer "shifts focus"–that is, how they move their eye muscles and change where they are looking–at the beginning of a new thought, and then sustain their gaze on that focus for the duration of the thought? The best singing actors have a strong, expressive gaze (a "thinking eye"), good ocular mobility, and the ability to coordinate focus and thought-to "match the gaze to the phrase," as we say in SAVI talk.

So, how's *your* "eye language"? Use a video camera to record yourself while you're singing and pay particular attention to your eyes when you watch the results. Do they seem glassy and blank? Does your gaze wander randomly while you sing? Do you gaze rigidly at a fixed point for a long time? Do you blink excessively or close your eyes while you sing? Power, expressiveness and control of the eyes are all technical skills that can be cultivated through deliberate practice.

I recommend spending a few minutes of your workout time conditioning the eye muscles in preparation for expressive singing. Here are some useful activities to incorporate into your workout:

- Squeezing the eyes tightly shut
- Opening the eyes as wide as possible
- Winking, blinking and squinting
- Moving your eyeballs up and down and from side to side
- Searching or scanning the room with your eyes, as if you're tracking a flying insect or searching the room for a clue

Be attentive to the muscles that control your gaze as well as the muscles around the eye that control your eyelids and the "squint" muscles below the eyes. Squinting is a common, unconscious side effect of vocal effort that makes you seem vague and shy. It's important to practice singing with your eyes fully open to maximize your expressiveness.

EXERCISE: Silent Eyes

Practice using your eyes alone to send each of the following messages silently:

- I'm happy to see you!
- What's wrong? Is something bothering you?
- I know what you did-you're guilty!
- I didn't do it, I'm innocent!
- This is really weird!
- Wow, you're really attractive!
- Get away, you're scaring me!
- Do you understand?
- That question you asked makes me very uncomfortable.
- I'm so proud of you!

Say the words of each phrase to yourself (like verbalized subtext or an "inner monologue") while looking at a partner or the lens of the video camera, then look at the playback or get feedback about how well you succeeded in conveying the message. You'll find other phrases in the SAVI Subtext Cards; you can also try using phrases from songs you know, or even "paraphrases," where you put the gist of a lyric into your own words, and then "transmit" them as messages with your eyes. Now practice your use of "eye language" while speaking and singing, using phrases of sung or spoken gibberish or vocal exercises while "transmitting" behavioral messages with your eyes.

The "One-Two" Focus Shift

Knowing how to use the muscles of your eyes to control and coordinate your focus-that is, where you look while you're singing-is a crucial skill you must master as a singing actor. You must have the ability to look wherever you choose for as long as you need to, and know how to change focus in a way that delineates the behavioral changes and inner thought processes embodied in the structure of a song or speech. In order to create the kind of phrase-by-phrase specificity that good singing-acting requires, you must develop the ability to change or "shift" your focus when a new phrase, thought or idea begins and then sustain your new focus for the duration of the phrase.

A delicate, subtle coordination of the movement of the head and eyes is required to make a change of focus seem lifelike and believable. Research has shown that the parts of your brain that control the movement of your eyes are the same regions of the brain you use when you shift attention. Careful observation of everyday life shows that, when a new thought or stimulus gets your attention, your first response is to move your eyes. It's a response that requires no conscious decision or awareness on your part. If you hear or sense something, your eyes will seek it out and begin to move in that direction. A moment later, your head will turn and your body will adjust, following the impulse that began with your eyes. Any new idea or impulse is accompanied by the same pattern of response.

I refer to this two-step procedure as a "one-two" focus shift, using the terminology of the teacher who first brought it to my attention, Wesley Balk. It's something we all do instinctively in real life, but you're probably one of the many singers who don't use it on the stage. Instead, many tend to rely on a single focus for much longer than seems natural. This phenomenon of "eye lock" is the unintentional result of concentrating very hard on your singing and making an intense effort to "do a good job" as a performer. Practicing the one-two focus shift as part of your daily routine, therefore, is a really smart thing to do. It may seem mechanical or even silly at first, but once you've mastered it and learned how to use it at the right times, it will bring a whole new level of authenticity, power and clarity to your onstage communication.

It may not have occurred to you, but adding focus shifts can enhance your onstage performance in much the same way that "cutting" from one shot to another adds interest to a film or video. When you move your eyes to a new focus, your spectators are likely to ascribe meaning to that change. Subconsciously they recognize that the moment after the focus change is different from the previous moment, and some part of the spectator's brain will try to puzzle out what makes the new moment different. This is very similar to our experience watching a recorded image, where a change to a new angle or shot in a film seems to add meaning and richness even though the subject being photographed remains the same.

The "one-two" focus shift is simple to practice, and you can do it almost anywhere. To begin, focus your gaze on a specific spot in front of you. Holding your focus steady, say the word "And..." aloud (or silently, in your inner monologue) to put yourself in a state of readiness. Next, when you're ready, move your eyes (and only your eyes) to look at something else, letting them dart as quickly as possible to that new focus. As you do that, say to yourself, "One," quickly and sharply. A brief moment later, allow the position of your head and body to adjust so that you're now facing the spot your eyes landed on. As you make that adjustment, which should be easier and more gradual, say to yourself, "Two," imagining a more sustained, relaxed tone: "Twooooo."

"And..."	*"ONE!"*	*"Twooooo..."*
	(quickly, all at once)	*(with ease, smoothly)*

If you're practicing in a group, it's the leader's job to say "And... one! Twoooooo..." If you're working alone, you can say these prompts aloud or think them silently. You'll hear these prompts used on the pre-recorded track I've made for practicing this exercise.

Practice this a half-dozen times or so, varying the time between repetitions randomly between three and ten seconds. Then relax before trying another round.

EXERCISE: Coordinating Focus and Music

Once you've gained some proficiency with this two-part move-ment of the eyes and head, it's time to practice coordinating the "one-two" focus shift with some musical phrases. The content-neu-tral "ABC Song" is a great piece to use for this.

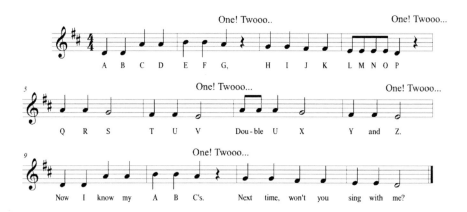

This familiar children's melody is made up of six two-mea-sure phrases, and I've marked where the "one-two" shifts occur in between each phrase of the music. (If you're up for a challenge, you can divide measures five through eight into four one-mea-sure phrases, each of which should begin with its own focus shift.)

Once you've got the hang of coordinating the one-two focus shift with the timing of the music and the beginning of each new phrase, try adding an additional behavior choice immediately after "Twooooo," accompanied by a count of "Three." The new behavior can be a change of facial expression, a change of body language, an adjustment to your vocal sound, or any combination of those elements.

Here's where your SAVI Cards will be super useful. As you prepare to do this exercise, lay out a few different cards and quickly commit the sequence to memory. I recommend memorizing the sequence because you're working on using your eyes as part of the exercise, and if you also have to use your eyes to look at the cards to remember what comes next, it will interfere with your progress.

As an alternative to memorizing the cards, you might tape your SAVI Cards on the wall instead. Tape the cards to the wall at your eye level, and spread them out in a way that will allow your focus to shift from one card to the next using the "One-Two" pattern you've practiced. Once you've begun the exercise, shift your focus from one card to the next and adjust your behavior as soon as you see the prompt on the card.

Another good SAVI étude to use for practicing the One-Two and One-Two-Three focus shifts is the song "I Have A New Idea."

The ding that I've marked after the word "idea" bears a closer look. Let's take a closer look at the sentence structure of the lyric:

> I have a new idea,
> A thought I must explain.
> And I can keep explaining
> Without a sign of strain.

You'll notice that the clause "a thought I must explain" is not a complete sentence by itself. It's there to elaborate on the word "idea", as if to say, "Let me tell you more precisely what I mean when I say 'idea.'" It's not an entirely new thought; rather, it serves to modify what was said previously.

This is a great example of an "And" ding. Since the second line functions both as a continuation of the first line and a modification of it, it probably doesn't make sense to use a One-Two focus shift here, only an adjustment of behavior. As you work on this practice song, try it both ways, with and without the focus shift.

EXERCISE: Numbers on the Wall

A variation on this exercise that will help you achieve a strong and articulate focus involves small squares of paper (sticky notes work great) with consecutive numbers written on them. Choose a big wall in your practice room and stick the numbers all over it in random order in different locations. Position the numbers at different heights: some at eye level, some up near the ceiling, and others down lower.

Now stand facing the wall and, using the "one-two" focus shift pattern, locate each number in turn. Go in ascending order, then try going from the highest to the lowest number. Sustain your gaze on each number for a few seconds. Vary the duration of your gaze randomly, from two to ten seconds, making a point of keeping your gaze alive for the duration of the phrase.

Once you've gotten the hang of it, coordinate these focus shifts with a vocal exercise, a content-less song (like the "ABC Song") or a piece of repertoire.

Summary

The quality of your singing-acting will take a big leap forward if you condition your face so that it's supple, strong, and articulate enough to express a thought or emotion. Expand your repertoire of facial expressions by imitating examples from real life. Practice "matching your gaze to the phrase" with "one-two" focus shifts, and incorporate decisions about how you'll use your face and eyes into your performance plan. If you want to take your singing acting to a whole new level of expressiveness, remember, "your face is your ace!"

CHAPTER 9

Voice and Music Choices

I love great singing of all sorts: show tunes, classical art songs, opera, jazz, rock, contemporary music. My personal taste skews toward unique voices and unique vocal ensembles, but I have an appreciation that borders on reverence for great singers in all genres. Singing, regardless of whether it's plain or fancy, raw or refined, is a glorious expression of the human spirit.

Singing musical theater is uniquely challenging because the literature is so incredibly varied. Many singers specialize in a particular genre based on the kind of music they prefer. You'll need to get yourself some "big ears" as quickly as possible, though, because as a singing actor, you'll be called upon to sing in all sorts of styles across your career. If you're too specialized or narrow in your tastes, you could well be limiting your future opportunities.

The SAVI System was developed in an environment where students were getting voice, dance, acting, and musicianship training, but needed extra help putting these ingredients together. One thing I saw time and again was that my students were hesitant to move beyond singing to singing-acting; that is, they were acquiring the skills they needed to produce a beautiful sound, but there was a need for provocation, for disruption, in order for them to create behavior.

In the vocal studio, teachers and students alike sometimes become focused on the goal of creating an "ideal" sound. Wesley Balk coined the playful acronym "OOPS" as a term to debunk the idea there is "One and Only Perfect Sound." What's OOPS about that? Well, oops, sorry, but there's really no such thing, at least not when it comes to singing onstage.

If there's an ideal to be pursued in musical theater singing, it's the ideal of adaptability, the ability to adjust your vocal production to serve the needs of the moment. Balk had another acronym for that kind of sound: UBU, which stood for "Unusual But Useful."

The remarkable array of sounds we can make when singing makes it hard to find language to use when talking about singing that will feel universally relevant. I'm not going to write about vocal technique in this chapter; I'll refer you to a few expert sources later on in the appendix, but I won't pretend that that's my wheelhouse. What I'd like to focus on in this chapter instead is the concept of **vocal behavior**, the choices that will make you a better communicator when you sing onstage. Exploring and expanding the array of "voice choices" available to you will make you a stronger singing actor, I guarantee it!

Does Your Voice Have a Voice?

Man, sometimes it takes you a long time to sound like yourself.

—Miles Davis

The term "voice" isn't used just to refer that audible thing we use when singing and speaking. When a writer is said to have a "voice," the noun refers to the distinctive and unique way she or he has of expressing themselves in written language. There's no mistaking James Joyce for Ernest Hemingway or Shakespeare for David Mamet, and so we use the word "voice" to refer to the distinctive traits that identify a particular writer.

In the world of singing, many of the best-known singers have distinctive characteristics that make their identity immediately recognizable. Streisand? Sinatra? Jolson? Pavarotti? Tom Waits? Janis Joplin? Insert the name of your favorite singer, and then ask yourself, *What is it about that singer that makes their sound identifiable and distinctive?*

Time and again, I've heard directors, music directors, and casting directors working in the theater speak of their desire to hear "authentic" voices. The industry continues to have a desperate need for voices that have "voice." The good news is, in the theater, you don't have to sound like anybody but you. But there's a catch: many traditional roles from the repertoire are identified with a particular sort of sound, such as Barbara Cook's clear-as-a-bell soprano; the big, brassy Merman-ish belt; or John Raitt's baritenor. As you train for the musical stage, you'll work with teachers who are experts in cultivating one or more of those styles, but the goal, ultimately, is not for you to be a carbon copy of any of these great singers. It's to find your_own voice.

The Goals of Vocal Training

Much of the work done in the vocal studio is designed to prepare students to replicate existing models of singing. This is understandable, given that a great deal of the repertoire is established and that the path to employment in the field involves preparing yourself to slot into certain existing categories or types of singing. If you can duplicate the sound and style of Jennifer Holliday, you can slot into roles like Effie in *Dreamgirls*; ditto Idina Menzel and the role of Elphaba in *Wicked*, and so on.

Listening and imitating existing models is a well-established form of training, and if you're not doing it already, it's certainly worth a try. It may be that the singers who excite you are not singing musicals, and it's fine if you want to model yourself on Britney Spears or Michael Bublé rather than Barbara Cook or John Raitt. In the course of your training, it will be advantageous to familiarize yourself with the sounds of singers who were successful and highly regarded for their artistic achievements, because this helps to cultivate a sense of the potential forms of excellence that artistry can take.

Along the way, however, you also need to discover your own voice. While there's unarguable value in knowing and admiring the voices of others and allowing yourself to be inspired by those voices, the musical theater needs singers who can convey authenticity and individuality in their sound. Often, these are the voices that composers want to write for. When new work is created, it is tailored to the vocal qualities of the individual singer. Kurt Weill often spoke of how he composed melodies with the voice of his wife and muse, Lotte Lenya, in his imagination. Unique voices like Carol Channing and Elaine Stritch have inspired composers to craft songs and roles especially for them, and Jason Robert Brown fashioned the leading role in the musical version of *Bridges of Madison County* to the vocal abilities of Kelli O'Hara. With this in mind, part of your goal should be to be the singer on the original cast recording, the one that other singers want to imitate.

When you work on your voice, you and your teacher should ideally strive for a balance of these two aspects: preparing your voice to sing existing repertoire in a way that matches existing models, and discovering the distinct individuality in your voice that makes you unique, inimitable, one of a kind. The work will be a mixture of digging deeply into the types of music that excite you and arouse your artistic passion and of thoughtfully exploring other types of music and roles that you may not be familiar with, all in the expectation that you will discover new sounds and styles to excite you and make you more versatile and employable.

Regardless of the style in which you are singing, there are five fundamental outcomes that will always be a part of vocal training for the musical stage.

1. Emotional expression, with intensity. The musical theater dramatizes characters in situations where they are confronted with extremely challenging circumstances. Inevitably, as a singer you will be called upon to sing with authenticity in situations that are emotionally charged: with excitement, with anguish, with desire, with rage. The language of emotional intensity varies widely from genre to genre: "Piece of My Heart" and the Mad Scene from *Lucia di Lammermoor* couldn't be more different in their vocal technique, but they both call upon the singer to convey emotional intensity.

2. Vocal health and stamina. Singers in the musical theater are called upon to sing a piece of material over and over again in rehearsals and performances. Rehearsals can vary in duration from a short coaching session to a full day's work, and a working singing actor can be called upon to perform eight or more shows a week. The singer needs the ability to deliver the goods consistently, again and again.

3. Versatility, range and flexibility. Work written for the musical stage invariably requires a certain amount of range and versatility even within a single show. Ensemble members are often called upon to play different characters during the course of a show, while characters playing leading roles are seen in different circumstances, singing different styles with different emotional qualities. What's more, over the course of a career, a singer will need to compete successfully for a variety of roles and shows.

4. Musical accuracy, from memory. The singer is responsible for executing the creation of the songwriter and the arranger in a manner that will satisfy its creator(s) or the members of the creative team on the particular production for which they've been hired.

5. The ability to make behavioral choices while singing. As Axiom 1 states, "When you sing onstage, your job is to create behavior that communicates the dramatic event phrase by phrase." Musical theater singers need to cultivate creativity, originality and artistry in their ability to make behavioral choices that illuminate the soul of the material, the individual who is singing, and the dramatic circumstances.

Fear of Music

Those readers hoping for a Talking Heads tribute here are going to be disappointed. Instead, I'd like to pose a question: As a singing actor, do you need to read music? What about sight singing and music theory?

College training programs for the singing actor generally include a year or two of musicianship and sight singing. In fact, several of my colleagues have authored texts specifically oriented toward the needs of the singing actor, using musical theater literature rather than classical music for examples and curating the topics covered to those most relevant to musical theater performance. Of course, getting an A in musicianship is no guarantee that you'll have success booking a gig. Once you're on the gig, though, you'll earn the admiration and gratitude of the composer and music director if you bring good musical skills to the work, which contributes to an efficient and positive rehearsal experience. If you get a reputation for being a good musician, it'll serve you well when those creators are hiring again.

It's been my experience that singers who understand the fundamentals of music theory-notation, intervals, rhythm, solfeggio, melody, basic harmony and song form-are more confident and independent when learning new music, especially choral music with vocal harmonies, and more sensitive and intelligent when it comes time to interpret a song. The converse is true as well: students who struggle, for whatever reason, with these subjects may well find themselves insecure and worried when faced with new music—in a callback, say, or preparing new audition repertoire, or even in music rehearsals for a show. This can translate into physical tension and emotional issues of self-worth.

There are plenty of singing actors who don't read music and still enjoy successful careers. Still, there's a persistent stereotype in the industry that singers are, as a rule, inferior musicians compared to instrumentalists. (Q: How can you tell when a singer is at the door? A: They can't find the key, and they don't know when to come in.) Dancers, I fear, have an even worse reputation when it comes to music skills.

Do you want that kind of reputation to follow you around? A SAVI singing actor will learn enough musicianship to be able to pick up new repertoire quickly and interpret it thoughtfully. Your musicianship skills will be a secret superpower as you analyze the phrases of a song, recognizing cadences, motifs, rhythmic and melodic patterns, and melodic contour.

For this reason, it's worth incorporating some musicianship work into your daily practice. Singing with solfeggio and singing different intervals and scales can be easily incorporated into your vocal workout. Singing in harmony and counterpoint should be a part of a performance class experience whenever possible. These kinds of activities will make you feel increasingly like a native speaker of the language of music.

Training the Hybrid Singer

Do you need to take voice lessons to be a successful singing actor? These days, the answer is almost certainly "yes." With upwards of a hundred colleges and universities turning out students with a BFA in musical theater each year, the odds are that anyone waiting in line with you at your next professional audition will have had several years of voice lessons at a minimum. More likely than not, they saw their voice teacher for a lesson or a tune-up only a few days ago. So yes, I think you need voice lessons, but let's make sure you're getting the right sort of lesson.

Great singing isn't just about what happens in the vocal folds, though; it's the product of an exquisitely coordinated effort of body, mind and spirit, and so the contemporary voice teacher needs to be conversant in topics like posture, breathing, and neurology, along with vocal anatomy. In recent years, voice science has made enormous advances, giving us invaluable data on vocal function and suggesting ways that function can be improved through scientifically grounded therapy.

Singers and voice teachers are, in my experience, a remarkably generous group of colleagues, always looking for ways to make best practices available to students and singers everywhere. I know a vast number of committed pedagogues, many of them friends and colleagues, doing invaluable work in the field. Their backgrounds, though diverse, usually include some sort of foundational training in classical technique, but over the years, they've learned to adapt their bel-canto foundation in response to the unique stylistic demands of the modern repertoire, often because they're facing those challenges in their own performing careers or because their students need to be able to sing in styles where old-school technique just doesn't seem to do the trick.

The emphasis of much current training is wellness, and contemporary teachers want to pass on to their students the key to a healthy voice. Many incoming musical theater freshmen exhibited some sort of **phonotrauma**, some way in which their vocal production was problematic. It is startling to survey the range of pathologies they present, including reflux, vocal fatigue, and the consequences of intubation during anesthesia. If you are a singer who exhibits symptoms like this, you need a teacher who knows how to help rebuild a damaged voice or, at the very least, one who will refer you to a qualified specialist.

Complementing the growing awareness of voice science in vocal pedagogy is an awareness of the psychology of learning and training. Voice teachers have borrowed the concept of "motor learning principles" from exercise physiology to help singers develop a productive practice regimen, one that can serve not only the development of good singing but also good singing-acting—that is, the effective coordination of the singing voice with the face, eyes, body, and other "organs of expression."

Audio technology is yet another frontier for the contemporary voice teacher to confront. Voices are rarely heard nowadays without the intermediating presence of a microphone and amplifier system. Voice teachers with experience working in the recording studio have been able to provide insights into what every singer and singing teacher needs to know about microphones and signal processing, and are pioneers in their efforts to introduce audio technology into the voice studio.

A good voice teacher will be an invaluable guide and companion on your journey to becoming a SAVI singing actor. If you're a voice teacher, I salute you in your ongoing efforts to serve all the needs of the modern "vocal athlete."

Musical Behavior and Musical Choices

It's important to realize that you're going to be making a lot of musical choices as you develop your own personal interpretation of a song. You'll probably do that in consultation with a conductor, a music director, a coach or accompanist, and maybe even the songwriter. Sometimes you'll even get to propose your own ideas or make your own decisions.

Some composers are more painstaking than others in the level of detail they provide in a musical score, and the level of detail in the musical score you're working from can differ substantially, depending on which edition of the song you are using. Is it a composer's manuscript? A Broadway show score? A version published in the "vocal selections" or downloaded from an online service like MusicNotes.com? A lead sheet? All of these are legitimate resources you could consult to learn a song, but all will vary considerably in the amount of musical information they provide.

If the score you're working on is painstakingly detailed, the product of a meticulous composer, consider yourself fortunate. However, now it's up to you to translate those musical details into dramatic life. You'll have to decide why the composer marked a *crescendo* here, a *sforzando* there, not to mention the staccatos and fermatas and other fancy Italian music words.

It turns out that songs are exceptionally malleable and that transforming songs musically is part of the everyday work of the musical theater. In my opinion, one of the characteristics of a great song is that it can be sung in a variety of ways, making it a new work even while it retains many of the familiar qualities that make it beloved. Part of being an artistically savvy singing actor is knowing how a song can be transformed and having the creative confidence to do so when the opportunity presents itself.

What kind of music choices will you face when working on a musical theater song? Here are six for you to consider.

1. Tempo. Sometimes a song comes with a metronome marking, which is a very specific way for the composer to indicate his preference as to how fast or slow the song should be sung. You may decide to follow that metronome marking, or perhaps you won't. Sometimes songs are marked with descriptive words that require some interpretation: How fast is *allegro*? How moderate is *moderato*? Will you try to copy the tempo on the original cast recording? (In this case, consider that often those tempos have been altered in the recording process.) Bottom line: tempo is a choice. Consider your options, and choose thoughtfully. Then, be sure to take the time to communicate tempo carefully when you're singing with an unfamiliar accompanist.

2. Key. Back in the day, the key of a song was fixed and non-negotiable. With the advent of transposable online sheet music, though, it has become increasingly common for singers to be able to choose the key in which they will sing. If you're singing in a published show with a published orchestration, you won't have that option, but rental houses like Music Theater International offer "transposition on demand" services. There are a small army of folks with Finale skills only too happy to put your song in a new key or make a custom arrangement for a small fee. So, there are many occasions when key is a choice, and that means you'll have some say in where a song will "sit" on your voice. This has significant consequences for what kind of effort you'll use to sing and how the song will align with your vocal identity.

3. Routine and road map. Are you singing the full song or an audition cut? Will you sing all the verses in the specified order? In a production of a standard title, you'll have little say in the matter, but you'd be surprised how many shows actually require some creative decision making about which songs and which verses to perform, and in what order.

4. Dynamics and articulations. You'll find plenty of *pp*'s and *ff*'s in well-edited published scores, but not as many in lead sheets or songbook editions. Regardless, there are plenty of decisions still to be made about dynamic details not spelled out in the published music. As for articulations—those little salt-and-pepper marks including staccato marks, tenuto marks, accents, fermatas, and railroad tracks-you and your conductor or coach will probably sprinkle them liberally over your score. Always have a pencil handy, and always, always mark up your music!

5. Modifications of the written music. Should you riff or not riff? Back phrase or sing on the beat? Swing those eighth notes or sing them straight? What about adding an extra high note or a fermata to show off your amazing voice? What about a whole new arrangement, with a different accompaniment, a different style, a different groove? There's an amazing array of possibilities to discover once you come to realize that no song is carved in stone, not really. Even the ones that seem very set-Bernstein, Sondheim, Weill, LaChiusa, Guettel-have been modified and reinterpreted when the occasion calls for it.

6. Lyrics. Did you know that many songs have different lyrics in different editions? What you find online won't match what's in the Broadway show score, songbook editions often vary, and many songs have unpublished alternate lyrics.

Thinking of musical choices like these as "behavior" enables you to build a closer relationship from moment to moment between the dramatic event and the musical score. Treat the composer's dynamic markings and articulations as guides to emotional expression, and approach your musical score not as something to be slavishly followed, but rather as something that can be adjusted, creatively and respectfully, in support of your interpretation. Add a fermata here? An accent there? A modulation in the final chorus? A riff, an alternate note, a rhythmic variation? These are the things that will make your performance distinctly yours, different from anyone else's.

As with so many aspects of singing-acting, we arrive at the best results through an iterative process of experimentation-try one choice, then another-and selection. The SAVI études in this book are a great platform for free experimentation. Every practice session should include time for you to try out different options, a process that will be made easier with the useful prompting of the SAVI Cards.

EXERCISE: Breath Work

Before there can be tone, there must be breath, moving dynamically through the vocal folds.

From the first moment of birth, breath is essential to life. Most of the time, we don't give a thought to our breathing; it is managed for us by the body's nervous system in ways that require little or no conscious thought. Changes in your physical and emotional state unconsciously alter your breathing patterns. Your rate of breathing might speed up if you're frightened or halt temporarily if you're hyper-focused on a task. Mastering the breath and using it consciously is a fundamental skill that gives the singing actor a way of calming the nerves and creating emotional expression.

Most voice methods pay considerable attention to the use of the breath in singing. Efficient phonation, vocal intensity and the cultivation of a smooth, connected (legato) tone are all achieved by cultivating a skillful use of breath. Often, a singer is confronted with the challenge of finding places to breathe in a piece. Identifying those places correctly and breathing strategically are part of the successful preparation of a vocal music performance.

Inhalation. Conscious inhalation begins with an impulse or an idea. You think of something you want to say, and as you do, the muscle of the diaphragm contracts, creating a vacuum in the lungs that causes air to be drawn in. This causes expansion of the chest, and a good, full breath will stretch out the intercostal muscles and the ribcage. As the diaphragm contracts, it moves downwards, pushing against the organs below it. As you consciously inhale, release the abdominal muscles (the belly) to create some space for those organs to move into.

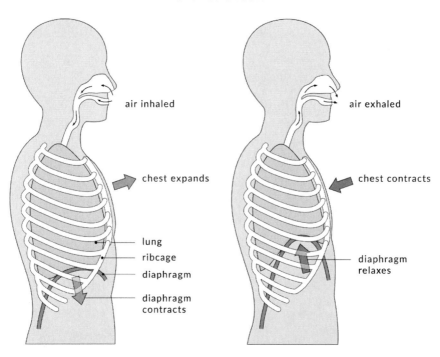

air inhaled

air exhaled

chest expands

chest contracts

lung
ribcage
diaphragm

diaphragm
relaxes

diaphragm
contracts

Exhalation. When you exhale, you release the muscles of the diaphragm you used to pull the air in. For the singer, though, it's not enough to simply release the diaphragm to create the dynamic, regulated airflow required for effective phonation. The singer also activates the abdominal muscles, which were relaxed during inhalation, to push against the organs behind those muscles, which in turn press against the diaphragm and propel the air in the lungs back out. A regulated exhalation without phonation—in the form of a slow hiss or a series of short pulses—is a good warm-up exercise to activate the abdominal muscles.

Different muscles come into play during the twin phases of inhalation and exhalation. During inhalation, the diaphragm contracts and the abdomen releases; during exhalation, the abdomen contracts and the diaphragm releases in a balanced, coordinated manner.

The SAVI Workout introduced earlier on page 58 offers ways you can activate the muscles that you use in your breathing process to create a more dynamic, balanced use of the breath. Here are some additional things that can be done alone or in a group to explore your use of the breath.

Pulsing the breath. Release the abdominal muscles and allow a generous breath to fill your body. Release the breath on a slow, steady hissing sound (/s/). Use your abdominal muscles to create a rhythmic pulse in that sound. Create a rhythmic pattern, such as four sixteenth-note short pulses followed by a long, steady quarter-note hiss:

/s/ /s/ /s/ /s/ /sssssss/

Capacity and flow of breath. Vocal exercises that start with short phrases and grow longer, such as this one, are good for working on capacity and flow of breath:

Do

Do re do

Do re mi re do

Do re mi fa mi re do

Do re mi fa sol fa me re do

Do re mi fa sol la sol fa mi re do

Do re mi fa sol la ti la sol fa mi re do

Do re mi fa sol la ti do ti la sol fa mi re do

Continue the exercises using the descending scale, starting on a high do:

Do

Do ti do

Do ti la ti do

Do ti la sol la ti do

Do ti la sol fa sol la ti do

Do ti la sol fa mi fa sol la ti do

Do ti la sol fa mi re fa sol la ti do

Do ti la sol fa mi re do re mi fa sol la ti do

Try singing this exercise in a canon with a group; it sounds terrific! Whether you're singing in a group or singing alone, this exercise is great for practicing the coordination of focus and breath. You can substitute numbers for solfège syllables, and use minor scales as well as major.

"Counting chords." This is another group exercise that addresses the individual singer's ability to maintain a steady flow of breath while also addressing ensemble singing skills. Your teacher will divide the group into different vocal parts and assign each part a different pitch in a chord. For example, basses and altos might sing "do," while tenors sing "sol" and sopranos sing "mi." Have the group intone their assigned pitches as they count "one-two-three-four-five." Then change the pitch by a half-step up or down, and make the phrase one count longer. Continue to adjust pitches and add to the length of the phrases until you've reached the group's limit.

As with the exercises in the previous chapter, you can get double the benefits if you incorporate focus work into counting chords. Choose a new focus and/or facial mask as you take a breath before initiating a new phrase. I also like to randomize the phrase lengths in this exercise; that is, as my singers are breathing and preparing for a new phrase, the leader will call out a number that will specify the length of the new phrase. With a little adroit coordination from an accompanist, you can also vary keys randomly rather than moving by half-steps.

Breath work with SAVI Cards. The previous exercises focus on building up breath capacity and the physical coordination required for dynamic inhalation and exhalation. You can also work on the behavioral qualities of your breath to discover that you can actually incorporate "breath behaviors" into your creative choice-making.

In his book *The Theater and Its Double*, Antonin Artaud writes, "every mental movement, every feeling, every leap in human affectivity has an appropriate breath." Later in that same book, he adds, "Breath accompanies the feeling, and one can penetrate into the feeling by the breath, provided one has been able to discriminate which one corresponds to what feeling."[24] Susana Bloch was inspired by Artaud's example to incorporate a deliberate use of breathing patterns into the Alba Emoting™ pedagogy as a way of inducing emotional states.

Experimentation with the relationship between breath and sound can be done alone in the practice room or with the guidance of an instructor. Choose a SAVI Phrase Card, each of which has a strong emotional component, or create one or more short phrases of your own. Experiment with different types of inhalation before the phrase:

- a quick, sharp "startled" in-breath
- A slow, steady, sustained in-breath (deep and long)
- Several quick panting breaths in and out (quick and shallow)

In each case, explore what impact a specific choice of inhalation has on the phrase that follows.

EXERCISE: Exploring Vowel Sounds

A good tone begins with a dynamic breath, but it's in the vocal folds where breath becomes tone, the result of a process called phonation. It takes a coordinated use of the resonant space in your throat, mouth and nose to amplify the tone created in the vocal folds and shape it into the many different vowel sounds that singing requires of us.

In spoken and sung English, there are a dozen single vowel sounds (monophthongs), plus a number of combination vowel sounds called "diphthongs" and "triphthongs." We learn these vowel sounds as we learn how to speak, imitating the sounds we hear around us. Later in life, you may choose to relearn these vowels to cultivate a "neutral" way of speaking that is free from regionalisms. It helps to learn the International Phonetic Alphabet (IPA), which includes symbols for all vowel and consonant sounds,

---

[24] Antonin Artaud, *Collected Works*, Vol. 4, trans. Victor Corti (London: Calder & Boyars, 1974), 101, 103

many of which are not easily represented using the 26 letters of our alphabet.

If you know the musical *My Fair Lady*, then you're familiar with Shaw's fictional phonetician Henry Higgins and his efforts to give Eliza Doolittle a speech makeover. The way you talk gives listeners strong signals about where you're from, how educated you are, and what social and economic class you associate yourself with. Just like Eliza, you may find the speech habits you acquired growing up can limit the kinds of roles you can successfully play, and that mastering a non-regional dialect and the IPA will give you greater versatility and improve your opportunities.

This sentence is a "phonetic pangram" incorporating all of the "pure" monophthong vowels in English:

Who would know aught of art must learn, act and then take his ease.

The "vowel ladder," created by Kristin Linklater, a highly regarded teacher of voice for the stage, uses these same sounds in a slightly different order, coordinated with a series of body movements, to develop resonance and a strong connection between body and voice. Google it and try it for yourself!

Diction for the Singer

Vowels are indisputably important to the singer; they provide the emotional heart of any singer's tone. Consonants, however, play an equally important role in singing, in that they are essential for clarity of communication and the successful delivery of information. Good diction is crucial for intelligibility and "putting over" a lyric.

You can make diction another one of your secret singing superpowers if you use the following three tips to give those consonants the attention they deserve in your training, conditioning and practicing routine:

1. Get to know them all. A good curriculum for the training of singing actors should include a class in voice and speech that familiarizes you with the consonants, the symbols used to represent them, and the parts of your anatomy that are involved in producing those sounds. Here's a somewhat simplified consonant chart with keywords in English:

Lips	Lips & Teeth	Tongue & Teeth	Tongue & Gum Ridge	Tongue & Palate	Palate	Velum	Glottal
p "pop" b "bob" m "mom" (w) "win"	f "fan" v "van"	th "thing" TH "then"	t "tot" d "dad" s "sass" z "zap" n "nan" l "little" r "roar"	sh "shoe" zh "casual" ch "church" dzh "judge"	j "Johan"	k "cake" g "get" (not "gem") ng "sing"	(glottal stop) "uh-oh" h "hey"

Voiceless consonants (p, f, th, t, s, sh and k, for example) do not involve phonation (tone produced by the vocal folds) but require energy in the breath. Voiced consonants (b, v, TH, d, z, zh and g are the voiced counterparts of the previous list) require you to produce a tone as part of the sound, and one of the best ways to make your singing more expressive is to bring more voice to your voiced consonants.

2. Conditioning in the practice room. Tongue twisters are a great place to begin your diction warm-up. Try speaking and singing phrases like:

The tip of the tongue, the teeth, the lips…

A box of mixed biscuits and a biscuit mixer.

You know you need Unique New York.

Red letter, yellow letter. Red leather, yellow leather.

A proper cup of coffee from a proper copper coffee pot.

A quick search on the internet will turn up scores of phrases like this, all designed to stimulate and challenge the use of your muscles of articulation.

I also recommend deliberately incorporating consonants into your vocal conditioning work. For example, here's a favorite vocalise of mine, a simple pattern of descending thirds (sol-mi-fa-re-mi-do-re-ti-do).

First, sing the phrase on a vowel sound without consonants. Then add an initial consonant, as shown in the second example above, taking care to get the tone going in the consonant sound before you open to the vowel sound (for example, "Mmmeh"). Begin the consonant sound slightly before the beat so that the vowel arrives on the beat. In classical singing, take care to ensure that the pitch you make on the initial voiced consonant is the same pitch as the vowel that follows it; varying the pitch of the initial voiced consonant can be used to create useful stylistic effects, and the practice room is the perfect place to explore these options. Choose different voiced consonants from the consonant chart above ("Vvveh," "Zzzeh," "Thhey," etc.) and use pitches that are both high and low in your vocal range. This sort of vocal exercise can sharpen your awareness of the different categories of consonants and the different parts of the anatomy they involve: the lips, the tongue, the teeth.

Final consonants, the ones that appear on the back end of words, deserve some love in your vocal warm-up and conditioning sessions, too. Learn to carry your vocal energy all the way through a final consonant and even a little bit beyond it, creating a neutral (**schwa**) "shadow vowel" as you vocalize using practice phrases like "Come home," "My love," or "Good news!"

3. Detailed work on a single phrase. After you've spent time getting all your articulators ready for action, choose a single phrase from a song you're working on or a practice phrase like the one below.

Kiss me, squeeze me, drive me cra - zy!

Remember that you need to understand every single word in each phrase you sing, not just its dictionary definition, but also what it means to you in context. Apply onomatopoeia to your phrase, choosing a quality for the sound of each word that is congruent with its meaning. ("Rough" should sound rough, "gentle" should be sung gently, and so on.) As you practice singing the phrase, take care to ensure that the voiced consonants have plenty of tone, the voiceless consonants use a generous amount of breath, and your initial consonants are timed so that the vowel is heard on the beat, not after the beat. If your phrase has diphthongs in it (like the word "drive" in the practice phrase above), be sure to sustain the first vowel of the diphthong, not the second (drAAAHHHeeve, not drahEEEEve). Slow the phrase down and concentrate on enunciating the text fully before bringing it up to tempo.

Increasing the intensity of your diction requires that you mobilize your face. Explore the results you get when you combine a strong choice of facial expression with heightened diction.

If you are working on this in a class, imitation and repetition are useful ways to explore different levels of intensity in diction behavior. The Call-and-Response exercise described below is a useful procedure for bringing greater intensity to your diction or any aspect of your vocal performance.

EXERCISE: Conducted Vocalise

When you and your classmates "conduct" the phrases of your vocal warm-up, you'll discover a simple but powerful way to awaken interpersonal communication and deliberate choice-making.

Decide on a phrase or simple pattern of pitches for the vocalise; my default choice is usually a pattern of descending thirds:

Arrange the group in a circle to start, and designate one member of the group to conduct first. The job of conductor should be given to each member of the group in turn; this can be accomplished if the role of leader travels around the circle every few phrases. The conductor gets to control key attributes of the vocalizing. For instance, when does the phrase begin? How fast or how slow should it go? How loud, how soft? Legato or staccato, accented or not?

Conductors should be encouraged to lead the expressive act of singing, not just mechanically "beat time." Going to expressive extremes, in the exaggerated manner of a conductor like Leonard Bernstein, is to be encouraged. Face, eyes and body should be active when the conductor leads. In fact, you can suggest that the conductor lead the group without using their arms or hands, a constraint that will compel the leader to be more physical and facial.

Each leader, when it is their turn to conduct, should be encouraged to have a strong idea or concept in mind before starting the phrase. SAVI Cards are a useful source of ideas for this exercise! Having the conductors change choices between phrases and having different conductors lead the exercise in turn will contribute to the quality of specific, varied choice-making during the vocalizing.

Once the group has successfully mastered the coordination this activity requires, give each conductor two SAVI Cards and have them conduct two phrases in succession, with the quality of each phrase dictated by one of the two cards. Each student gets the experience of choosing and changing, as well as leading the group through a moment of transition and change.

You can use other music in Conducted Vocalise; "The ABC Song" and "Row, Row, Row Your Boat" are simple songs for a warm-up or beginner session. The vowel pangram song "Aught of Art" introduced above would be a good choice for this exercise, too, and if you're feeling adventurous, there's really no music that can't be explored in a group with a creative conductor.

EXERCISE: Vocalise and Songs with SAVI Cards

The SAVI Cards are an invaluable way to introduce new ideas and "voice choices" into your daily personal practice. Choose a handful of SAVI Cards-some adjectives, some action verbs, some musical descriptors-and select a new card just before you begin a new phrase, incorporating that prompt into your vocal sound. This is as valuable when working on vocal exercises as it is when exploring a piece of repertoire.

EXERCISE: Call-and-Response

In a group class, this exercise based on a traditional "call and response" pattern can help the group develop a wide range of vocal behaviors.

Start by having the group stand in a circle. One member of the group should sing a short phrase, then everyone else in the group should echo that sound. The phrase can be anything: a bit of vocalise, a phrase from a song, a gibberish phrase or even a bit of text (the SAVI Cards include a number of useful phrases) set to an improvised tune. Then, have the next individual in the circle sing solo, and have the group echo their phrase. Give each person in the circle a SAVI Card prompting them to make a particular voice choice, perhaps an Adverb Card ("harsh," "gentle," "timid," "bold") or a Music and Voice Card to incorporate in their singing.

As a variation, use a "three-peat" process with the call-and-response exercise:

1. The soloist sings and the group echoes that phrase.
2. The soloist sings the phrase again, choosing some aspect of the phrase to intensify. (More intimate? More staccato? Raspier? More beautiful?) Often the sound the group makes will inspire the soloist to go further with some particular aspect of their singing. It's as if the sound of the group singing the individual's phrase serves to magnify or amplify that phrase, making it possible for the soloist to exaggerate some quality in their sound just a little bit further. After that, the group echoes the enhanced phrase.
3. Repeat the process again (or even more than three times), using the back-and-forth process of the soloist and group and the process of exploration and intensification for as long as they seem useful. Then go on to the next soloist.

Summary

Chapter 9 is meant to get you to thinking about what you need to do to "sound like yourself," in other words, to find a way of singing that expresses your personal essence. The concept of the "hybrid singer" is introduced as a way of discussing the many challenges you'll face as a singer whose mandate is to communicate the dramatic event through sound and music. The exercises presented in Chapter 9, many of which involve the SAVI Cards, are meant to cultivate a more expressive use of breath, vowel tone and diction and a more creative approach to the notated musical score.

CHAPTER 10

Body and Movement Choices

Every little movement has a meaning all its own,
Every thought and feeling by some posture can be
* shown.*

– From *Madame Sherry* (1910)
by Karl Hoschna and Otto Harbach

Having considered the face and the voice in our examination of behavior, we now turn to the third of the expressive modes, the body. The idea of expressing yourself through "body language" is probably a familiar concept to you. When you looked at videos of performances with the sound off (see Chapter 7, page 89), you probably got a great deal of information from the performer's body language.

However, as we found with face, eyes and voice, if your "vocabulary" of body language is limited, there's not much you'll be able to say, and unless you have some understanding and control over the language of gesture and movement, the messages you send via your body language are likely to be confusing. In this chapter, we'll explore some ways to use gesture and movement with greater specificity and greater variety.

Good movement training for the actor consists of "considerably more ... than simply training an actor to be a 'fit' person or a veritable virtuoso of performance skills,"[25] says Anne Dennis in her book *The Articulate Body*; "... we are not simply talking about the actor who can somersault through space or who can perform a mean tap dance..."[26]

Instead, she envisions an approach wherein "...each part of the actor's instrument [must be] tuned to respond to all internal and external influences; and these responses must be visible to the audience. The basis of the actor's craft is to reflect through his physicality all that is happening inside: to make the invisible visible."[27] I find particularly compelling her presentation of the idea of diction in an actor's movement vocabulary-the need for articulation, emphasis, and even punctuation in the pursuit of clarity of behavior.[28]

Types of Gestures: Face, Space, Body, Partner

With such a remarkable array of gestures available to us, why is it that so many singers stand with their arms lifeless at their sides, or rely on a single gesture over and over? SAVI technique work invites you to consciously explore a variety of gestures as part of your practice. Mind you, I'm not saying that your limbs should be constantly in motion when you perform. It is natural for young performers who discover the liberating feeling of being "allowed to" gesture to use too many gestures in their performances. With practice, you will find you are able to gesture whenever you choose to, and that when you choose to, you'll have an interesting array of gestures to choose from.

Where's a good place to begin to build your gesture vocabulary? I suggest you start with real life, or with photographs of people in real-life situations. What kinds of gestures do they use? Start a Pinterest board where you collect images of gestures that inspire you. Look at images from a variety of sources, pictures of people "performing" as well as people in the midst of their daily lives. Do "performing" and "non-performing" gestures have

25 Anne Dennis, The Articulate Body (London: Nick Hern Books, 2002), 8.
26 Ibid., 18.
27 Ibid., 19.
28 Ibid., 44.

different qualities? Try copying some of both types of gestures and consciously incorporating them into your warm-up and conditioning work. When you put on those gestures, do they make you feel any different?

To begin to expand your gesture vocabulary, look for gestures that fall into a range of categories. In particular, I've found it helpful to consider these four specific categories of gestures:

1. Gestures that refer in some way to your own body: hands on hips, hand on heart, thumb pointing to chest ("Body" gestures);
2. Gestures that refer in some way to your face: touching the face with the fingers or palm, hiding the face behind the hands, running your fingers through your hair ("Face" gestures);
3. Gestures that refer in some way to a partner, either real or imagined: pointing, waving, beckoning ("Partner" gestures);
4. Gestures that relate in some way to the environment and the space around you, without regard for a specific person ("Space" gestures).

In your private practice sessions, move randomly between gestures in these four categories (Body, Face, Partner and Space) as you vocalize. A group class is also a great way to explore gestures and to share gestures through a process of initiating and imitating.

The Mirror Canon exercise that we introduced in an earlier chapter is a great tool for exploring gesture in a group setting. This exercise calls upon you to choose a gesture for each phrase, either by initiating a gesture for your partner to imitate or by imitating a gesture that your partner has initiated. As you perform the Mirror Canon with different partners, do you find yourself initiating the same handful of gestures over and over again? If so, deliberately introduce the four categories of face, body, partner and space; try doing the Mirror Canon using one of the four categories for each of the four phrases. There are also four SAVI Cards for these four categories to help you mix up the categories in group or private practice.

The Psychological Gesture

Acting teacher Michael Chekhov developed a tool called the Psychological Gesture, which is currently taught by many acting teachers. The nephew of the famed Russian playwright Anton Chekhov, "Misha" was considered by Stanislavski to be his most brilliant pupil. His approach to gesture is presented in detail in his books, *To The Actor* and *On The Technique of Acting*. His students learned to develop a signature "psychological gesture" (PG) as a way of embodying the unique attributes and personality of a character, as well as additional PGs that could serve to define the physicality of particular beats or actions in a drama. Chekhov made a strong case for the "psycho-physicality" of actor training; that is, he understood that the inner life of the actor and the outward expression of that life in gesture and movement had a duplex relationship, each affecting the other.

As part of his work, Chekhov identified 10 "archetypal" gestures: **push, pull, lift, smash, gather, throw, penetrate, tear, drag,** and **reach.** Actors working in his studio found that these 10 different types of movements activated their imaginations and emotions in especially useful ways.

In your practice room or in a studio setting, you can begin to experiment with and explore these categories, first working with movement alone, then incorporating these movements with vocal phrases or phrases from songs. The SAVI études "Come to Me" and "Get Away from Me" (introduced in Chapter 6) are excellent places to begin to explore the archetypal gestures of Pull and Push, respectively. As a preparation for singing "Come to Me," experiment with a strong gesture of pulling something toward yourself; you can also make the gesture more "veiled" by "pulling" with your gaze or your inner monologue. Prepare for "Get Away from Me" by repeating strong gestures in which you forcefully push something away from yourself; internalize the emotion you experience with this gesture through your inner monologue and your gaze to explore the "veiled" version of "push." Use the SAVI étude "More and More" (described in Chapter 16) with its musical variations to explore the archetypal gestures of Gather and Throw.

Fake It 'til You Make It

Psychologist Amy Cuddy received a great deal of attention a few years back when she originated the idea of "power posing." She became widely known for a 2012 TED talk called "Your Body Language May Shape Who You Are,"[29] in which she talks about the idea of **postural feedback**, a term that describes how your emotions are actually affected by the position of your body when you adopt a certain sort of posture or stance. Her research made the case that "power posing"—that is, adopting a stance associated with a powerful individual (a wide stance, direct eye contact, chin lifted, etc.)—can make you feel more confident. In fact, this feeling of confidence appears to be linked to higher levels of testosterone, a hormone associated with confidence, and lower levels of cortisol, the hormone your body produces under stressful situations.

Dr. Cuddy's research has particularly significant implications for women, and she speaks persuasively about her own personal experience and the value this approach has had for women who employ it. While the scientific community continues to debate the validity of her research, there is a great deal of anecdotal evidence to suggest that a conscious use of gesture and posture can strongly influence an actor from the outside in.

Are you a young singing actor who struggles with issues of confidence? As we peer at our phones and computer screens, we become accustomed to a bent-over posture that robs us of a sense of personal power. The physical language of "power" and "powerlessness" are clearly recognizable even to the untrained

---

[29] Amy Cuddy, "Your Body Language May Shape Who You Are," Ted Conferences, LLC, June 2012, www.ted.com/talks/amy_cuddy_your_body_language_shapes_who_you_ are.

observer. The poet Maya Angelou writes, "Stand up straight and realize who you are, that you tower over your circumstances. You are a child of God. Stand up straight."[30]

EXERCISE: Gesture Shopping

Seriously, who doesn't love shopping? You know what they say: "When the going gets tough, the tough go shopping."

Gesture shopping can be used both for "work on the singer" and "work on the song," which we will get to shortly, in Chapter 12. It will expand your behavior vocabulary during warm-ups and workouts, and supply you with "proposed" behaviors, ideas for gesture and body language to support specific moments in your songs. Gesture shopping is guaranteed to deliver a creative jolt, whether you're feeling stumped and stuck or interested in taking your work to a higher level. Gesture shopping was developed as a classroom exercise and works well when you have even a small group of three or more students. I'll start by introducing several versions of gesture shopping that you can use in a classroom, and then go on to describe some variations using video sources or observational fieldwork that you can do on your own.

If you stand in a circle with a view of your classmates, it's stimulating and useful to exchange gestures while you vocalize or warm up. Working in a circle is a great opportunity to practice both initiating and imitating behavior. As you're about to begin a phrase, you should choose one of these two options: either select someone from the circle whose body language you're going to imitate, or decide to initiate some choice of body language for others in the circle to imitate. During the course of the warm-up, switch frequently between initiating and imitating.

This procedure is easily adapted for use when a solo singer is working in front of a group. For the exercise to be effective for you as a soloist, you'll need to have broken the song down into "dings" ahead of time. Present your song once or twice if your

_____

[30] Maya Angelou, *Rainbow in the Cloud: The Wisdom and Spirit* of Maya Angelou (New York: Random House, 2014), 58.

classmates don't already have a general familiarity with the piece and its behavioral requirements. Now recruit a few members of the class to serve as "models." Their job will be to stand and face the singer in places where they can be easily seen; usually, I set this up with the models standing in front of the first row of seats in the classroom, in between the soloist and the remaining spectators. The models' assignment is to choose gestures and body language that support the material and the diversity of moments in the song. When you sing, their job is to present their proposals wordlessly to you as soloist as you sing the song. You will choose one (and only one) of the models at the beginning of each phrase and quickly adopt and copy their physical behavior (gesture or movement) as they sing. With each new ding, choose a behavior proposal from a different model and/or have the models make new proposals about the physical behavior that could accompany the current phrase.

Gesture shopping is a psycho-physical exercise, not just a thoughtless mimicking of random poses. For the exercise to be fully effective, all participants must be willing to internalize the emotional life of the song and its moment-to-moment fluctuations and to explore the ways the inner life and external behavior of the singer can be linked. Encourage a fierce commitment and interaction on the part of all participants. Make sure the behavior changes at the dings have a lively, ouch-y quality. Consider using video to document the models in the gesture shopping session for repeated use in a solo practice session.

There are ways to put the creative power of gesture shopping to work for you even if you don't have access to a class or group setting. Here are two of my favorites.

"Gesture Shopping" Variation #1: Online Shopping. We live in the age of the internet, a media-saturated environment in which you have infinite access to images and footage from both historical and casual sources. If you're playing Eva Perón or Charlie Chaplin, for instance, you've got a trove of visual sources from which you can choose behavioral and gesture ideas. But try searching Google for images using any keyword (an emotion, a name, whatever), and you'll be amazed at the useful models you'll find. Even Instagram will have useful ideas to offer, and Pinterest is a convenient online resource for compiling and curating behavioral ideas that you find into an inspiration board.

"Gesture Shopping" Variation #2: Gesture Shoplifting. Ideas for behavior can be found all around you, not just online. Your friends, your family, even strangers can be potentially valuable sources of ideas for gestures and other specific behavioral choices. Good ideas for gestures and behavior will present themselves at unexpected moments if you're alert to those opportunities. You don't even need to ask permission to use them; just help yourself! Keep your eyes open and have a notebook or note-taking app handy to record great ideas when you encounter them.

Stillness and Movement

As you prepare to sing a song, one of the first things that makes an impression on your audience is your posture and stance. A good default stance is one where your feet are hip-width apart. Give your chest and shoulders a slight feeling of lift. Voice teachers often refer to this as a "heroic" stance.

Of course, not every song requires a heroic body image. If your song expresses a dejected attitude, your stance should reflect that. If you are confused or uncertain in your song, you should embody that state, but watch out that confusion and uncertainty in your stance don't undermine you in a song that is supposed to express confidence.

As a performer onstage, you'll need to be able to stand in a comfortable, energized way for an extended period of time. A change of stance, such as rearranging your feet to reorient your body without actually moving, can be an effective expressive choice at a moment in a song where you're beginning a new section or initiating a new action.

That's right, your feet aren't nailed to the floor when you sing! Movement in the space is a choice available to you at any moment in your performance, and can be especially useful at moments of transition. I find it particularly useful to explore what happens when you move to a new location at the beginning of a new phrase. Changes in the direction and quality of your movement that occur at the beginning of a new phrase are also useful to explore. During your SAVI Workout, I encourage you to explore what happens when you move about in the space while you sing.

CHAPTER 11

Input and Output

It's tempting to think of singing-acting as strictly output. When we sing and act, we make noise and create behavior and send them out to the other characters onstage and to the audience beyond it. But to achieve the peak performance skills of a SAVI singing actor, you must understand that **quality output requires quality input**. Just as we must inhale in order to exhale, we must take in information, sensation and emotion in order to express it in behavior. In this chapter, we'll explore the crucial importance of input to the singing actor, introduce the concept of "ouchability" and explore some strategies you can use to achieve a better balance between input and output.

Come to Your Senses

"Come to Your Senses" is the title of a Jonathan Larson song that became part of his posthumous show, *Tick, Tick... Boom!* In the show, Larson's song is sung by a woman trying to awaken the feelings of a man she cares for, but I find the message to be powerful and useful for the singing actor, too: if you want to take your singing-acting to an elite level, you need to *come to your senses*.

Choreographer Agnes de Mille had the same thing in mind when she declared that she wanted dancers in her musicals to be **sentient**, capable of feeling and perceiving. The etymology of the word sentient reminds us that "sensing" and "feeling" are closely related, and therefore are distinct and separate from "thinking" as a form of mental activity. Sight, hearing, touch and proprioception are all critically important to you as a singer and an actor; even your sense of smell can exert a surprisingly powerful influence. Sensations can influence you in the present moment, but remembered sensations can also be quite powerful; Stanislavski was keenly interested in the power of "affective memory" and how remembered sensations affect the emotions.

When you learn to "come to your senses," to activate your senses of sight, hearing, smell, touch and proprioception, your ability to connect with the dramatic event in the present moment will increase. You will be better able to create behavior that is specific, authentic, varied and intense. Your senses are the way you engage with the world around you, the real world as well as the imaginary world of the play. Without that engagement, your work as a singing actor won't be as good-or as SAVI-as it needs to be to succeed.

Sending and Receiving

A successful conversational requires you to be a good listener as well as a good talker, doesn't it? Nobody likes to talk to someone who's not listening. When we have lines to say onstage, though, we put a lot of effort into memorizing those words and saying them correctly. It's understandable that speaking might require more effort than listening. When your words are set to music, the challenges of learning and delivering them are considerably greater, as is the likelihood that the effort devoted to those tasks will preoccupy you entirely, leaving no "mental bandwidth" for listening.

In an interview about singing and acting, soprano Natalie Dessay acknowledged that challenge: "It's almost impossible to sing and really act at the same time.... For me, acting is receiving, and singing is giving, and that is why it is so difficult, because your mind does one thing and your body does another."[31]

Acting teachers and directors understand how important it is to listen as well as talk. Hearing and seeing what your partner says

[31] Rebecca Mead, "The Actress," *The New Yorker*, February 22, 2009, www.newyorker.com/magazine/2009/03/02/the-actress.

and does and responding to that behavior is essential to believ-ability. It's simply unnatural to have one without the other. This give-and-take, this ebb and flow is all part of the natural rhythm of nature, like waves coming in to the shore only to wash back out to sea. But if it's so natural, why is it so hard?

The main problem is the nature of song, which not only requires hard work to learn and deliver but often takes the form of a soliloquy. In many songs, you are alone onstage for a period of minutes with no scene partner, no one to serve as a vis-à-vis, except perhaps the audience on the other side of the footlights. In the score of your song, the writer and composer have set down what is to be transmitted, but rarely give any indication of what's being received. That task is left to you as the performer, and you must use imagination and skill to fill in what they've omitted.

Unlike a conversation or a duet that simulates a conversa-tion, there's little opportunity for a natural give-and-take in a solo song. The relative proportion of singing time to listening/sensing/non-singing time is lopsided in a soliloquy. That means you've got to make the most of certain moments, of little breaks or cracks in the continuity of the communication.

In order to be able to breathe in and take in sensory informa-tion, it's necessary to *disrupt* the singing. This idea of disruption is a key step in coming to your senses. Disruption brings you out of your trance, like when the hypnotist snaps his fingers and you "snap out of" the hypnotic state. In singing, activating the senses is a way of restoring the balance between sending and receiving.

You need to be listening and responding regardless of whether or not you're the center of attention onstage. In a duet, this means the moments when you're listening are every bit as crucial as the moments when you're singing, and the same is equally true if you're a member of the ensemble. I'm sure you can recall the experience of watching two singers in a duet "taking their turns," counting their rests and following the score, all while failing to connect and failing to communicate. Whether you've got a short moment or a longer period of time when you're not singing, you can't just bide your time until your next musical entrance. You've got to be living in the moment, which means listening, seeing, touching, sensing in every possible way what's really happening in that moment, and letting yourself respond to that behaviorally. When you're hurt, you must flinch; when pinched, you must ouch; when acted upon, you must react.

EXERCISE: Following and Leading

Closely related to "sending and receiving" are the core concepts of "following and leading." In order to be a good follower, you have to pay attention to your leader, and you can't do that without using your senses. A responsible leader is always attentive to their followers, too, since it's crucial to know at any given moment whether your followers are with you.

A couple of exercises centered on the idea of leading and following can be very useful for helping you "come to your senses." The Mirror is a fundamental exercise that I first encountered through Viola Spolin's seminal book *Improvisation for the Theater*; I like the way it makes the abstract notions of the give-and-take in a dramatic situation more concrete and physical. The Conducted Vocalise exercise, introduced previously as a way of creating vocal behavior, has the additional benefit of making you pay attention to the others in the group rather than just yourself.

The Mirror and the Conductor exercises are both deceptively simple, but they provide a useful framework for discovering a greater quality of sentience in your singing-acting in a manner that is both playful and serious. Both exercises build focus and flexibility, and the experience of being both "leader" and "follower" is useful to the psychological development of the actor.

The idea of leading and following, initiating and imitating, can be explored by a larger group of participants in the "echo game," which Balk describes in *The Complete Singer-Actor*.[32] This game is built upon the concept of mirroring but alternates

---

[32] Wesley Balk, *The Complete Singer-Actor: Training for Musical Theater*, (Minneapolis, University of Minnesota Press, 1977), 116-118.

between the individual and the group. In this exercise, you should stand in a circle. One student makes a sound and the group echoes it, followed by each student in turn. In a second round, each student makes a movement with their sound, and the group copies both, mirroring the movement as they echo the sound. I encourage students to explore a spectrum of vocal behaviors (sung and spoken, gibberish and verbal), and sometimes give them single words or short phrases on cards for inspiration.

Any work that you do with a partner or in a group when you sing can make a meaningful contribution to the cultivation of sentient singing-acting. Keep this goal in mind when you're fortunate enough to be singing in a group. Notice what the others are doing and let yourself be affected by their behavior.

Get Ouchable!

To be human is to be **ouchable**, to feel the slings and arrows of outrageous fortune. As a child, you surely fell and hurt yourself and cried; you screamed with laughter when you were tickled; you wore your heart on your sleeve, and you were an open book where all your feelings could be read.

"Ouchable" is a deliberately playful term that I use to describe the physical and mental state of readiness, a feeling that you are poised to act or to react impulsively at the onset of a phrase.

There are several reasons why the quality of ouchability is crucially important to the singing actor. A singing actor who is ouchable is more lifelike, more natural and **more responsive to their scene partner and onstage environment**. Conversely, a singing actor who lacks ouchability is wooden, unnatural, less lifelike and less believable. The cracks, the disruptions, are how the life gets in.

When toy designer Caleb Chung created the Furby, he made several basic design decisions that played a key role in the toy's lifelike, "sentient" quality. First of all, he made Furby responsive to its environment. Furby creates the illusion of being interactive by being responsive to sensory information. Make a loud noise and

Furby will cry out; poke him and he'll laugh; turn him upside down and he whimpers with fear.

Like Furby, your sensors must be continuously active, taking in data from your environment. You must notice when things change so that the behavior you create can be responsive to that change. When you are ouchable, it enhances your ability to communicate the contrasting qualities in the successive phrases of a song. Ouchability enables you to make a new choice to support the onset of a new phrase, and every moment of change creates a richer and more complex sense of meaning in the mind of the spectator. Without ouchability, every moment becomes like every other moment: having the same focus, the same tone, the same general quality.

When is Ouchability Important?

While ouchability is a powerful attribute for the singing actor to possess, it may surprise you to know that you don't need to be ouchable all the time. There are certain moments in a song in which it is critical that you act or react, and you must learn to recognize them and treat them accordingly.

I thought about this phenomenon on a recent flight. I had put on a pair of headphones to block out the roar of the plane's engines and to listen to some music. As I saw the flight attendant approaching with her drinks trolley, I put my music on pause and removed my headphones for a moment so that I could hear her questions and place my drink order. At that moment, I knew I needed to be ouchable; that is, able to take in sensory information from my environment in order to make a choice.

Ouchability is most important at the dings, the moments when one phrase, action, or beat is ending and another is about to begin. It's like me with my headphones on the airplane: I took them off as the attendant approached, knowing that our interaction was about to begin and that the need to make a choice was imminent. Prior to that moment, it was perfectly acceptable-even useful-for me to remain under the headphones, not paying attention to what was going on around me.

Ouchability is less important, and may even be a liability, when you are in the middle of a phrase. Once a phrase has been launched, it's generally best to focus your attention on the phrase itself, playing the action and sustaining and developing the behavior you initiated to accompany your initial impulse.

What Diminishes Ouchability?

> *If you prick us, do we not bleed?*
> *If you tickle us, do we not laugh?*
> *If you pinch us, do we not ouch?*

> - With apologies to Shakespeare

To be ouchable, you must be in an unbraced physical state, unencumbered by tension, and likewise in an unbraced mental state, unencumbered by inhibition or fear. To "get ouchable" means to open yourself, to make yourself available and vulnerable to an impulse, a provocation, or an adjustment. Getting ouchable involves an intermittent occurrence, not a permanent transformation. The very notion of "ouch" is sudden, abrupt, convulsive—a quick and involuntary response to a specific stimulus, or a "pinch."

To understand the concept of ouchability more clearly, think of its opposite. Imagine you are in the dentist's chair, and you hear the words, "This may hurt a little." Or imagine you are about to get a shot in the doctor's office, and the nurse says, "You may feel a little pinch." As you imagine that situation now, notice how your body responds. You brace yourself, don't you? You tense up so that you won't flinch when the pinch finally comes.

Now think about an occasion where you had a strong reaction to something but needed to stifle your response—perhaps a formal or serious occasion where something funny happened—or an occasion where you thought you were alone and then discovered you could be seen and heard by others. Just allowing yourself to imagine such a situation is likely to produce a physical response of bracing and contracting in the body, accompanied by a self-conscious state of mind in which all responses must be suppressed.

When you are braced-up and tense like this, you are "ouch-proof" rather than "ouchable," and you'll probably exhibit some of these unwanted symptoms:

- Unresponsiveness
- Stiff, stolid, stuck posture
- Physically braced
- Locked eyes
- Tunnel vision
- Limited sensory awareness

Unfortunately for you as an actor, there are factors that diminish the innate "ouchability" you grew up with. At the very least, you should look out for the following:

- **Fear and inhibition.** Worry about being right or correct often leads to a lack of ouchability. It's useful to remember that I often coach a student to "Go ahead, mess it up."
- **Insufficient preparation.** This is a particular sort of fear and inhibition that is present when you have not practiced sufficiently. You are not secure in your memorization of words or music, or have not devoted sufficient time to exploring which behaviors might communicate the dramatic event.
- **Vocal discomfort.** When you encounter a passage that has extreme vocal demands or resides in a "problem" part of your voice (e.g., the passaggio or "break"), you will stiffen up as you physically and psychologically "brace yourself" for the challenge.

Becoming More Ouchable

Luckily, you can train yourself to become more ouchable. To begin, identify those moments in your song where it's important to be ouchable. These are likely to be critical moments that you can identify first by looking out for the dings in the piece. Identify those moments where ouchability matters and try some of these strategies as you approach them.

- Loosen up. Ragdoll, shake, shrug. Induce some movement in your joints.
- Ease up. Engage your Alexander Technique. Allow the whole head to move up and the neck to be free. Release your jaw, tilt your chin up and down slightly, turn your head left and right.
- Gurn. Flex your face. Induce some movement in your eyes and facial musculature. Look around.
- Activate your senses. Get outside of your head by directing your attention to your partner or your environment. Look and really see; listen and really hear.
- Find ways to surprise yourself and your partner. Decide to deliberately do something you haven't done before.
- Put in some "overs." Remember my analogy of an old war movie in which one soldier ends his statements on the walkie-talkie with the word "over"? It's understood that "over" means "I am done speaking, and now it is your turn to respond." Not only does this provide a prompt for a response, but it allows the speaker to switch over to a listening mode–to become all eyes and all ears. For the singing actor, an "Over" moment should include some sort of physical release. Ending a moment of communication entails allowing the effort you used in transmission to drop away, even if it's for a very brief moment before you pick it up again.

EXERCISE: The Tap

Physical touch has the power to create very strong emotional and biological responses, and the "Tap" exercise is meant to explore that power, cultivating ouchability and awakening the senses while singing. The Tap requires a minimum of two people, or a class organized into pairs. One person in each pair is assigned the role of singer, while the other is given the assignment of standing behind and occasionally disrupting the singer by lightly tapping them on the head, shoulders or body at the moment just before a new phrase is about to begin.

When introducing this exercise, especially with students who are younger and less mature, it's probably good to discuss the purpose of the exercise and set some ground rules. The "tappers" should understand that their job is to deliver a brief, useful disruption to the singer while remaining within the bounds of what the group agrees is "respectful touching."

As a preparatory step, have each pair stand in position with one in front of the other. Have the person in front stand in a relaxed, neutral manner, and instruct the person in back to deliver a "tap" (or touch or stroke) at random moments. Have the person in front notice whether they are unconsciously bracing themselves in anticipation of the tap. Is it possible to remain relaxed and engaged in the present moment even when you know a disruption is on its way? After giving the partners some time to explore this question, have them switch positions so that they both understand their respective roles and the responsibilities and challenges of each.

To make this work more specific, give the "tapper" some SAVI Emotion or Adverb cards to prompt them, using the word on the card to determine what sort of tap or touch to deliver to their partner. Because touch is such a powerful medium of communication, in most cases the person being tapped or touched will be able to correctly discern the quality of the touch without being told.

In the next stage of this exercise, add a vocalise or song will be incorporated into the work. Have the person standing in front get ready to sing a phrase, but instruct them to wait for a tap before they sing and incorporate any sensory information that comes from the quality of the tap into the way the phrase is sung. Once a phrase has been completed, the singer should wait for another tap before proceeding to the next phrase, and the tapper should try to randomize the duration of the pauses and the qualities of each successive tap. In this part of the work, it's important to work against any sort of preconceived tempo; the singer should be kept guessing about when it will be time to begin the next phrase.

During this part of the work, if you are a teacher or coach, pay attention to how the singer deals with the tap. Are they braced and unresponsive? Are they startled and overly responsive? Are they using the tap as an opportunity to take in new sensory information and make an adjustment as they initiate the new phrase? You will find it useful to coach both the singer and the tapper as they experiment with the idea of "productive disruption."

The singer and the tapper should work toward creating a continuous tempo while maintaining the element of surprise as much as possible. When is the most productive moment to deliver the tap? What is the most natural, useful relationship between the tap, the intake of breath, and the onset of the phrase? When you're doing this exercise, you'll soon discover that the "pinch" that creates your ouchability—in this case, the tap or other stimulus that initiates the phrase—occurs a few seconds prior to the start of the vocalization.

Summary

Chapter 10, the last in a series of chapters about "work on the singer," proposes that you consider the ways in which input is as important as output when you sing. **Quality output requires quality input, and to achieve this, sentience is key.** After examining some of the factors that make this a challenge, I introduced some exercises to help you get in the habit of taking in sensory information at the beginning of every phrase. Patient, persistent work on these exercises will eventually increase your available bandwidth to take in new sensory information and have it affect your behavior.

CHAPTER 12

Work on the Song

In the preceding chapters, we've explored skills that apply to every single song, regardless of style or genre, that you will use every time you sing onstage. I refer to this as "working on the singer" because, instead of preparing a song for performance, you are really working on yourself, mastering techniques that you will need when it's time to perform a song.

My focus in the following chapters will be how to apply those skills to specific repertoire and create a performance that has Maximum SAVI—that is, as Specific, Authentic, Varied and Intense as possible. The exercises and procedures I describe in the following chapters have all been field-tested and proven effective in the classroom and the rehearsal room. Follow the steps patiently, persistently and purposefully in order to take your work to the next level and attain your goal of peak performance.

Specimen Song for Analysis: "I'll Be Known"

I'm going to use an original song to demonstrate many of the procedures I recommend for repertoire preparation, or "rep prep," in the following chapters. Using an original song lets me speak authoritatively about the intent of the songwriter. I know this song won't be familiar to you, but approaching it without preconceptions, you'll get a better sense how SAVI procedures can work for you when approaching a new song. When you apply these procedures to a song you're preparing for a class, an audition or a role in a show, you'll gain valuable insights into the ways in which you can use behavior to convey the distinct essence of each individual phrase.

I've provided a lyric sheet and a vocal part with lyrics and dings for "I'll Be Known" on the following pages. A full piano-vocal score for this song can be found in the back of the book. You'll find a recording of a performance of this song, as well as a downloadable PDF of the piano-vocal score, at the Book Extras page on the SAVI Singing Actor site.

"I'll Be Known" is from the 2013 musical *Leading Lady*, which I wrote with playwright P. Seth Bauer. *Leading Lady* is the story of Mae Desmond, a famous Philadelphia actress who ran her own theater company, the Mae Desmond Players, in the early twentieth century. Born Mary Callahan, this daughter of Irish immigrants grew up in Southwark, a slum neighborhood of Philadelphia. The song is an example of what is referred to as an "I want" song, often found early in the first act of many musicals, where the protagonist sings of deeply felt desires that will motivate their actions in the events that follow.[33]

Even if you aren't able to listen to the song right now, you'll find you can learn a lot just from studying the lyric. To begin, let's examine the lyric without any sort of interpretative markup, just like you'd encounter it for the first time in the script:

> Growing up poor wasn't no picnic,
> Not when the cupboard was bare.
> Hand-me-down clothes, soup thin as water,
> And plenty of hardship to spare.
>
> One in a litter of shanty brats,
> Scratchin' and yowlin' like alley cats.
> Ten of us crammed in a Southwark flat.
> Well, I'll be damned if I'll live like that!

---

[33] For more on the convention of the "I Want" song, check out https://howlround.com/gimme-gimme. Jack Viertel's *The Secret Life of the American Musical: How Broadway Shows Are Built* is highly recommended if you want a better understanding of the construction of a musical.

I want more,
Aye, that's sure,
I'm gonna get it, I swear!

I want to be heard,
I want to be seen.
I want to be noticed,
Do you know what I mean?
I want to be known.

Known for my skill
Known for my craft
Known for my heart, my art--
Do you think that it's daft
That I want to be known?

There's plenty of kids in our family
But just one me
There's hundreds of girls at the factory
But just one me

There's thousands of faces like mine on the street,
Freckles and ginger hair,
But if somebody doesn't notice me,
I'll die, I swear.

A whiff of acclaim
Yes, that would suffice
Ah, hell, even somebody knowing my name would
be nice!

I won't just smile and pour the tea
And blend into the scenery.
I'll have a life
That I can call my own.
Perhaps I won't be famous,
But dammit,
I'll be known!

I'll Be Known

from "Leading Lady"

Charlie Gilbert

Grow-ing up poor was-n't no pic-nic, Not when the cup-board was bare. Hand-me-down clothes, Soup thin as wa-ter, But plen-ty of hard-ship to-spare. One of a lit-ter of shan-ty brats, Scratch-in' and yowl-in' like al-ley cats. Ten of us crammed in a South-wark flat. Well, I'll be damned if I'll live like that! I want more, Aye, that's sure, I'm gon-na get it, I swear.

I want to be heard, I want to be seen. I want to be no - ticed, D'-ye know what I mean? I want to be known.___ Known for my skill. Known for my craft. Known for my

I'll Be Known

C Piu mosso, with determination ♩= *84*

D As before ♩= *74*

E Emphatically, colla voce

heart, my art. Do you think that it's daft ___ that I want to be known? There's

plen-ty of kids in our fam-i-ly, ___ but just one me. There's

do-zens of girls in the fac-to-ry ___ but just one me. There's

thou-sands of fa - ces like mine on the street, freck-les and gin-ger hair, But if

some-bo-dy does-n't no-tice me, I'll die, I swear! A whiff of ac-

claim, yes, that would suf-fice. Ah hell, e-ven some-bo-dy know-ing my name would be

nice! I won't just smile and pour the tea and blend in-to the sce-ne-ry, I'll

have a life that I can call my own! Per-haps I won't be fa-mous, but

dam-mit, I'll be known! ___

Let's Break It Down

The language we use to talk about songs can be misleading. Consider, for instance, the song you've just looked at, "I'll Be Known." Everything that happens between the first and last measures of this song is collectively referred to using a singular noun ("a song"). This single unit has a title, a single phrase that, in this case, is the same as the final words of the song.

But is a song a single thing? Most definitely not! Axiom 7 of SAVI Singing Acting encourages you to "Learn to see a song as a journey, a series of events that occur in sequence." Breaking down the journey of the song into a series of clearly recognizable events is a core skill you must master as a singing actor.

In the next few pages, I'll break this song down into smaller and smaller units. Like zooming in on a map or a photo, you'll discover more details and greater insights as we increase the magnification. First, we'll look at the major sections of the song. "I'll Be Known" has five major sections, each of which has its own function in the song's dramatic journey. Within each of those sections, we'll find several stanzas. Finally, we'll look at how each stanza is made up of individual phrases and of individual moments in the song. Remember, your job is to communicate the dramatic event phrase by phrase, so this is where we'll really hit pay dirt.

As you break down a song in this manner, it may be helpful to think about the ways in which a song is like a book–even this one! The word "book" is a singular noun, a collective entity referred to by its title, but any book consists of multiple components that are organized sequentially. A book is divided into *chapters*, which are the equivalent of the major *sections* of a song. Each chapter is made up of a number of *paragraphs*, which are the equivalent of the *stanzas*. Paragraphs, in turn, are comprised of *sentences*, and *phrases* are the musical sentences from which a song is constructed. Every one of these levels of organization plays an important role in the way a book communicates its subject matter, and the same is true for a song.

Major Sections

Almost every song consists of a number of major sections. Songwriters use specialized terminology to describe these sections—for example, the verse, the chorus, the refrain, the bridge.[34] I'll provide definitions for and examples of these terms as we go, and I'll teach you to discern the important signposts that divide a song into major sections. For now, refer to the rehearsal letters and measure numbers to navigate the musical score in the analysis that follows.

A. The first section of this song begins with the first lyric, "Growing up poor" (measure 3), and ends after "I swear" (measure 24). The clearest indications that what comes next is a new section are the **performance instructions** that appear above the staff (*"Piu mosso,*[35] warmly") and the **double bar line** separating measures 24 and 25. The fact that measure 25 starts with a new **time signature**—moving from 6/8 to 9/8 time—is another indication that the following measures are a new section. However, please note that a change of time signature by itself doesn't necessarily mean a new section has begun.

This first section of the song is probably best described as the **verse**. Many theater songs include an introductory section like this to provide expository information and set the stage for the upcoming **chorus** or **refrain**. At the beginning, a brief instrumental introduction based on an agitated figure of sixteenth notes (you'll hear it in measures 1-2, and you can see it in the piano vocal version at the end of the book) establishes the key as A minor. I'll analyze the three stanzas of Section A when we zoom in closer later in this analysis, but for now, note how the third stanza, starting at measure 21, has shorter phrases, a simpler accompaniment and a slower tempo ("Slower, more freely"). This last part of the section serves as a transition to what follows.

---

[34] These terms are also used when a singer and accompanist are communicating during rehearsal. "Let's do the verse *rubato*, bass and drums come in at the chorus, and at the end we'll repeat back to the bridge."
[35] *"Piu mosso"* means "a little faster" in Italian. Using Italian for performance instructions is traditional, though sometimes it seems hard for an American composer to justify.

B. The second section begins at measure 25 ("I want to be heard") and ends at measure 36 ("...to be known?"). Notice how the same features—performance instructions, a double bar line and a change of time signature—serve to denote the beginning of a new section in the musical score.

Let's call this section the **chorus**, where the title phrase of the song will be heard for the first (but not the last) time. The chorus is direct and heartfelt and meant to be memorable in its simplicity; usually the chorus of a song includes material that will be heard several times before we're finished. This section has a different time signature and is in the key of C, the relative major of the preceding section, which was in A minor. The accompaniment, which consists mostly of chords, has a conspicuously different **texture** than the agitated sixteenth notes of Section A, and changes in texture are another important signpost of structure. The two stanzas in this section end with the words "I want to be known," a slightly modified version of the song's title.

C. The third section begins at measure 37, marked "*Piu mosso*, with determination," and ends after measure 44 and the lyric "I'll die, I swear!" This section has a different time signature (4/4 time, also known as **common time**) and tempo. In contrast with the previous section, the lyric has more syllables per line and a more rhythmic setting. It is common for songs to introduce a contrasting section, often called the **bridge** or **release**, after the initial musical idea of the song has been clearly established, and Section C serves that function in "I'll Be Known."

D. The fourth section, beginning at measure 45, is marked "As before," signaling a return to the chorus, the music heard in Section B. However, you'll note that Section D is only half as long as Section B. Measures 45-49 repeat the melody heard in measures 31-34, but instead of a second stanza, as in Section B, there is a quick transition to the fifth and final section.

E. The fifth section provides a **climax** and a dramatic ending for the piece. All the markers we have seen in earlier sections—performance instructions, a double bar line, change of meter and tempo–appear once more to signal the beginning of a new section. Starting at the pickup to measure 50, the music is marked "Emphatically, *colla voce*," a term that instructs the accompanist to follow the singer's tempo. A passionate exclamation and a climactic high note appear at the end, and the last word of the lyric is followed by an instrumental epilogue or **ride-out** that emphasizes the heroic fervor of Mary's final declaration.

The differing musical characteristics of these five major sections reflect their contrasting dramatic functions within the play. In Section A, Mary bitterly describes the difficult circumstances of her childhood. In Section B, she makes her first attempt to find words to describe her dream; she makes a couple tentative attempts before declaring, "I want to be known." In Section C, she compares herself to other girls her own age and voices her fear that she might be just another faceless non-entity. In Section D, she imagines how nice it would be to enjoy a "whiff of acclaim." In the fifth and final Section E, Mary boldly declares her intentions, with a shouted curse word and a held-out high note to create a dramatic climax at the end of the composition.

Not every song changes tempo or time signature with each new section. Indeed, many songs rely on a rhythmic "groove" or a flowing accompaniment that is continuous throughout the song, which can make it challenging both to discern the beginning of a new section and to create behavior that communicates that change in performance. Even if the musical texture is fairly consistent or continuous, the lyric of the song will reveal where the dings are, and you should use behavior to call attention to those places where the emotional journey of the song changes direction. Rather than surrendering to the groove, pay attention to the dings in order to create a performance that's "shish kebab, not applesauce!"

Stanzas and Phrases

Let's zoom in now and look at how each of the five sections of the specimen song can be subdivided into stanzas and phrases. As noted before, *stanza* is the term a lyricist or poet uses to refer to a group of phrases arranged in a pattern that will recur throughout the composition. When a lyric is written out separately from its music, the words are often arranged on the page in a way that is meant to make that pattern of phrases evident to the eye, with a blank line used to separate the end of one stanza from the beginning of the next. You'll find this to be the case with the lyrics of "I'll Be Known" on pages 174 and 175.

As previously mentioned, Section A consists of three stanzas. The first is a four-line stanza or **quatrain** in which the second and final lines rhyme ("bare"/"spare"). The second half of this first stanza ("Hand-me-down clothes/soup thin as water") provides specific examples of the hardship alluded to in the first two lines. The last line of the stanza ("And plenty of hardship to spare!") is a bitter joke in the same vein as Porgy's "plenty of nothin'" in the Gershwins' *Porgy and Bess*; that is, in a world where everything is scarce, the one thing to be found in abundance is suffering. This is an example of **wit**, a moment in which Mary makes a wry observation that calls attention to her own cleverness. Sometimes a character is unintentionally funny, but a witty line calls attention to the ingenuity of the character or the writer in some way.

The second stanza is also four lines, but is structured as a pair of **couplets**, two lines with end rhymes ("brats"/"cats," "flat"/"that"). The language is highly imagistic ("a litter of shanty brats," "alley cats," "crammed in a one-room flat"), as Mary provides colorful examples to add compelling detail to the story of her childhood. The descriptions build in intensity, growing increasingly vivid until the section reaches a climax and the busy accompaniment abruptly stops.

The third stanza is, as noted before, a transitional passage, three short lines in which Mary closes the door on the past and looks ahead to the future. For the first time, she speaks of her desires ("I want more") and her determination to achieve her dream ("I'm going to get it, I swear"). Fittingly, the music grows calm and determined, setting the tone for what follows.

Having declared "I want more," Mary now tries to find words to describe what she means by that in Section B. The first two stanzas of Section B have an identical form: a quatrain followed by a fifth line that serves as a refrain and is repeated at the end of each stanza.

I envision the first stanza as Mary attempting to find the right word to describe her ambitions. She tries out a series of words ("heard," "seen," "noticed"), considering the meaning of each in turn, but none of them satisfies her until she arrives at the last phrase, "I want to be *known.*" The pause that follows that word gives her a moment to think, "Yes, that's the perfect word," before she continues.

The second stanza is an attempt to fill in more details. Known for what? For skill, for craft, for heart, for art: emotional and musical momentum builds as the examples crowd into her thoughts. Suddenly, she experiences a twinge of doubt: "Do you think that it's daft that I want to be known?" "Daft" is an unusual word, not common in American English but colloquial in the British Isles, and it sounds perfect coming from the daughter of an Irish immigrant in the early twentieth century. I encourage you to be on the lookout for distinctive words like "daft" and give them a little something extra, a bit of behavioral emphasis so the listener can appreciate their special quality.

As you've followed along with my analysis, I hope you've imagined all the ways behavior could help communicate the particulars of the dramatic event I'm describing. I invite you to consider the remaining three sections on your own, letting your efforts be guided by these words of advice from novelist Vladimir Nabokov: "In art, as in science, there is no delight without the detail."

In the version of the lyric that appears below, I've marked a Δ symbol where each ding occurs; the lead sheet of the melody that follows also has the Δs marked. In the following chapter, I'll explain more about how to identify where each phrase begins. For now, see if you can discern the relationships between the phrases as you look through the remaining three sections. Read the lyric aloud, pausing at each ding to consider how the subsequent phrase differs from the antecedent phrase.

Δ   Growing up poor wasn't no picnic,
Not when the cupboard was bare.
Δ   Hand-me-down clothes,
Δ   Soup thin as water,
Δ   But plenty of hardship to spare.
Δ   One in a litter of shanty brats,
Δ   Scratchin' and yowlin' like alley cats.
Δ   Ten of us crammed in a Southwark flat.
Δ   Well, I'll be damned if I'll live like that!
Δ   I want more,
Δ   Aye, that's sure,
Δ   I'm gonna get it, I swear!

-----------(Section B begins)-----------

Δ   I want to be heard,
Δ   I want to be seen.
Δ   I want to be noticed,
Δ   Do you know what I mean?
Δ   I want to be known.

Δ   Known for my skill
Δ   Known for my craft
Δ   Known for my heart, Δ my art --
Δ   Do you think that it's daft
Δ   That I want to be known?

-----------(Section C begins)----------

Δ   There's plenty of kids in our family
Δ   But just one me
Δ   There's hundreds of girls at the factory
Δ   But just one me
Δ   There's thousands of faces like mine on the street,
Δ   Freckles and ginger hair,

Δ   But if somebody doesn't notice me,
I'll die, I swear.

-----------(Section D begins)-----------

Δ   A whiff of acclaim
Δ   Yes, that would suffice
Δ   Ah, hell, even somebody knowing my name would be
    nice!

-----------(Section E begins)----------

Δ   I won't just smile and pour the tea
And blend into the scenery.
Δ   I'll have a life
That I can call my own.
Δ   Perhaps I won't be famous,
Δ   But dammit,
I'll be known!

Analyzing the song in this manner—that is, by breaking it down into sections, stanzas and phrases—will help you discern the unique content of each phrase, the relationships between the phrases, and the overall musical and dramatic structure of the piece. These insights will prove to be invaluable as you memorize the music and prepare to perform the song.

CHAPTER 13

"Max S" (Maximizing Your Specificity)

Specificity is not only the first but in many ways the most important of the four attributes of effective singing acting described by the acronym SAVI. My examination of "I'll Be Known" in the previous chapter is meant to illustrate the kind of diligent effort and pains-taking attention to detail that is required when analyzing a song. Maximizing your specificity begins with analysis, but analysis must be followed by synthesis, as you make specific behavioral choices for each phrase based on your understanding of the song and the individual moments it is comprised of.

Understanding the Dramatic Event

Having a clear understanding of the dramatic event of your song is a crucial step toward maximizing your specificity.

In order to define the dramatic event, start with Stanislavski's **Fundamental Questions. T**he first three of these identify the so-called "given circumstances" of the moment, while the other four serve to situate your character within those given circumstances:

- **Who am I?** Physically, psychologically, both alone and in relationship to others.
- **Where am I?** Locale, environment, and your relation-ship to it.

- **When is it?** Time of day, year, season? Also, where am I in the arc of the story? What has just happened?
- **What do I want?** This is your goal or objective. Why do I want it? What makes it important? What motivates me?
- **What will I do to get what I want?** The answer to this question is best expressed in the form of action verbs.
- **What must I overcome to get it?** These obstacles serve to create conflict and intensify the struggle of the character.

Analyzing the text of a song is challenging because songs are highly compact, often formal or artificial in their structure, and they rely heavily on association, implication and poetic imagery. Effective song analysis will feel like a "forensic" process, like a detective piecing together clues. It often takes persistence and imagination to connect the dots and arrive at a vivid and performable understanding of the dramatic event of your song.

Sometimes a song will chronicle a single dramatic event, but it's not unusual for the dramatic event to change as a song unfolds over time. The start of a new major section or "chapter" in a song may be an indication of a change in the dramatic event as well. It is important to examine a song phrase by phrase and to discern the ways in which the individual phrases of the song differ from one another. With that in mind, let's add a couple questions to Stanislavski's list:

- **What's happening <u>now</u>?**
- And, most importantly, **how does the present moment differ from the previous moment (or moments)?**

"To Persuade" and Other Action Verbs

In the old-fashioned parlance of show business, a skillful performer was said to know how to "sell a song," a phrase that suggested that an energetic and earnest appeal to the listener was the key to a successful performance. I wouldn't be surprised if the crass notion of "selling" a song makes you cringe a little; in the lexicon of the modern-day *artiste*, such concepts seem frightfully *passé*.

As it turns out, though, many of the best songs in the musical theater repertoire involve an element of persuasion. Mama Rose tries (unsuccessfully) to persuade her father to support her show business dreams in the song "Some People" from *Gypsy*, and later puts a full-court press on her daughter Louise in the Act I finale, "Everything's Comin' Up Roses." Eliza Doolittle demands that Freddie be more demonstratively affectionate in "Show Me," from *My Fair Lady*, and Sky Masterson tries to cajole Lady Luck into not abandoning him in the climactic crap game of *Guys and Dolls* with his song "Luck, Be A Lady." Persuasion involves getting someone to believe or do what you want them to believe or do, overcoming any resistance they might have in the process, and this is one of the things songs do well in musicals.

When you examine a song in preparation for performance, see if you can detect an element of persuasion in the dramatic event. If you find it, be prepared to employ all available methods and tactics to "sell" your idea—that is, to persuade your onstage listener to accede to your wishes.

Not every song has a persuasive intent, but there is a specific component of dramatic action to be found in every song. Ask yourself the question, "What am I *doing* in this song?" The answer to this question should take the form of an action verb, and the SAVI Cards often a dozen action verbs to consider as you seek an answer to your question. If you're at a loss to come up with playable actions when performing your song, begin by experimenting with the different action verbs in the SAVI Card deck to see which ones feel promising.[36]

By way of example, let's consider some of the actions that Mary plays in the song "I'll Be Known" (presented in Chapter 12).

---

[36] There's also massive collections of actable verbs online at https://www.screenactorssystem.com/actable-verbs and http://texasartsproject.com/wp-content/uploads/2012/03/TacticList21.pdf.

- In Section A, in which Mary describes the difficult circumstances of her childhood, she seeks *to convince* her listener about the extent of the hardship she faced as a child.
- In Section B, she attempts *to describe* her dream and *to declare* her intention: "I want to be known."
- In Section C, she allows herself *to acknowledge* there are many girls just like her but takes pains *to assert* her own uniqueness.
- In Section D, she permits herself *to fantasize* about the pleasures of a "whiff of acclaim," then uses coarse language *to shock* her listener.
- In the Section E, the final section of the song, Mary's climactic actions are *to refuse* anonymity and to demand fulfillment of her dream.

All of the action verbs I've listed above–to convince, to describe, to declare, to acknowledge, to assert, to fantasize, to shock, to refuse and to demand–are dynamic choices that can be strongly conveyed through choices of face, voice and body. They provide an action through-line for the song that is specific and playable. By committing fully to each of these actions in turn, the actress playing Mary will achieve what Stanislavski referred to as the "reality of doing," a key component of believability onstage.

When it's time to persuade, don't be hesitant to "sell it, honey," but remember that you need to be ready to play a variety of dramatic actions.

Ding It Before You Sing It

The études in the first part of this book make each "ding"–the moments where one phrase or idea ends and the next one begins–very apparent. This was done intentionally to make it easy for you to focus your attention on the technical challenge of creating behavior in a way that coordinates with those changes. The location of the dings may be less obvious when you're analyzing a song for performance, though. Here's a quick tutorial on how to spot the moments where dings occur.

To do this work, get a copy of your song's sheet music you can mark up. This needs to be a different copy from the one your accompanist will use, since the marks you'll be making when you analyze your song will only confuse them. Once you have a private copy, feel free to mark it up to your heart's content!

It's hard to discern phrases when the lyrics are printed under the notes of the melody, but it can be helpful to see the way the lyricist lays them out in print in the script. When lyrics are printed as text in the libretto of a musical, they are usually arranged like verse, with a visual presentation that helps the reader see the rhythm and structure of the text and the way phrases are grouped into stanzas. If possible, try to find the text of the song as formatted by the lyricist, either in the libretto of the musical or in a collection of the writer's lyrics.

It is important to remember that *not every new line is a new phrase* when you are viewing lyrics in a published format. Punctuation and syntax are more reliable indicators of the onset of a new phrase. Again, for the people in the back: a phrase is not necessarily the same thing as a line of the lyric in print.

Here's a checklist of things to look for when you're identifying where phrases begin:

Punctuation: Periods, semicolons, question marks and exclamation points are clear indicators of the end of a phrase. A period signifies the end of a statement, as does a semicolon, while an exclamation point denotes additional emphasis or intensity. Questions make particularly good song lyrics, because they engage the listener with the expectation of a response.

Commas can sometimes mark the end of a phrase, especially when the next word is a conjunction or the next phrase has a parallel construction to the one before it. They also delineate the flow of thought in a lyric. Sometimes a comma will indicate the start of a new thought; sometimes it will indicate a parenthetical phrase, a detour from the current thought that will eventually lead back to the previous phrase; and sometimes it's just there to help you see the way that the thought is developing within the span of a single phrase.

Conjunctions: Linking words like "and," "but," "or," "however," "although," "except," "and yet" are particularly important signs of a ding. Think of these as *pivot words* or *hinge words* because of the way they indicate that the argument of the text is changing direction. A colleague of mine calls them "little big words": short and ordinary but full of power and meaning when they appear in a song.

Grammatical construction: The term *syntax* refers to the rules that govern the orderly construction of a sentence. Written language is expected to conform to conventional syntax, but conversational language is often more idiosyncratic. In songs that deviate from conventional syntax–like Amy's frantic soliloquy "Getting Married Today" from *Company* or Candela's "Model Behavior" in *Women on the Verge of a Nervous Breakdown*)–new thoughts often begin unexpectedly, derailing the previous train of thought. By closely following the flow of such a stream of consciousness, you can discern the onset of new thoughts even when the character's state of mind is disorderly.

Rhyming words: Though not all rhymes denote a ding, they are often used in combination with other items on this list to call the listener's attention to the end of a phrase.

In addition to paying attention to grammar and syntax, one of the most helpful things you can do to identify the dings in your song is to write or type out a copy of your lyrics separate from the music. There are several schools of thought about how to organize these lyrics. Some think you should write them out like a poem, with the lines laid out according to their rhythm and rhyme; this is usually the way they'll be presented in the printed script or on a lyrics website. Others say it helps to write the words out in a paragraph without line breaks to help you think about the text of the song like a speech or a monologue rather than a poem. I recommend a middle ground that incorporates aspects of both approaches. That is, I suggest you write out the lyrics so that each phrase of the song appears on its own line. This will make it visually apparent where each new phrase begins when you study and organize your lyrics for performance.

Finally, here's a tip you'll find enormously helpful when breaking a song down into phrases: start with the last phrase and work your way backwards. Since the end of the song is inarguably the end of the last phrase, work your way backwards from the end until you find the beginning of that phrase. That'll be the moment when the penultimate (or next-to-last) phrase ends, right? Now work your way backwards to the beginning of that next-to-last phrase; that moment will be the end of the previous phrase, and so on. Combine this technique with a careful use of all of the items on the checklist above, and soon identifying the dings in your song will be one of your secret SAVI superpowers.

Marking Up Music

Examining the lyric of a song is only part of the work you need to do to prepare. The musical score of the song also contains vital information that will contribute to a successful, expressive performance.

Do you mark up your music? If you don't, you are missing out on one of the most important tools available to help you maximize your specificity as a SAVI singing actor.

Every singing actor's "book" contains copies of sheet music, neatly prepared for the convenience of the accompanist and marked with performance instructions, but that's not the type of marking up I'm referring to. Along with the copy that's in your book, you need a working copy of your song, a *secret* copy upon which you can work out your ideas about your performance.

A page of sheet music is full of information, though, and it can be a challenge to separate the important information from the distracting details. For the singer, the most important information will be found on the staff where the melody and lyrics appear. I'm not suggesting that the accompaniment in the sheet music is irrelevant—-it merits study, to be sure—-but the most useful information will typically be found on the top staff, where the vocal melody appears.

Here are some things to include when you examine the music of your song:

1. **Key and scale.** Is your song in a major key or a minor one? Does it change from major to minor, or vice versa? Some commentators ascribe certain qualities or "colors" to specific keys. Sharp keys, for instance, are thought to be "brighter," while flat keys are "richer" and "mellower." Does the song change keys? It's common for a song to modulate to a higher key as its emotional intensity builds to a climax.

2. **Melodic contour.** The term *contour* refers to the rise and fall of the pitch in the melody, and often will vary noticeably from phrase to phrase. Examine the contour of each phrase, looking out for places where pitches are repeated, where pitches move by steps, and where they move by *skips* (intervals of a third) or *leaps* (intervals of a fourth or greater). Generally speaking, big leaps in the melody are a sign of dynamic forces at work.

3. **Rhythm and prosody.** Do the words (or some of them) tumble out in a flurry, like in Sondheim's "Getting Married Today"? Does the rhythmic setting deliver the text in a steady, stately way? Are there long, sustained pitches? Dotted rhythms that create an uneven, skipping quality? Tempo and rhythm regulate the speed at which a song delivers information to the listener, and so the relationship between the lyric and the fundamental beat of the music is an important indication of the emotional life of a phrase.

4. **Long final notes.** A long, sustained note followed by a rest is the most common musical indication of the end of a phrase.

5. **Cadences.** Composers often use a progression of two or three chords called a **cadence** to create a sense of completion or resolution at the end of a phrase. Cadences often end with the **tonic triad** (the "I" or "One" chord that corresponds to the key your song is in) or the **dominant chord** (the "V" or "Five" chord, whose root is five steps higher than the tonic). It's worth knowing enough musical theory to be able to recognize the common cadences that signal the end of a phrase.

6. **Harmonic rhythm.** Harmonic rhythm refers to the rate at which the chords change in a composition, or in other words, how often the harmony changes in relationship to the measures and meter of the song. Harmonic rhythm is likely to vary within a composition, sometimes even within the individual phrases of a composition. The harmonic rhythm of a song helps to determine the listener's perception of how static or dynamic the character's state of mind is at any given moment.

7. **Dynamics, articulation marks and other performance instructions.** This category includes adjustments in loudness, accents that emphasize key words, staccato marks that make the individual words short and detached, and phrase marks (**slurs**) that instruct you to connect one pitch smoothly to the next. There's a wide array of words (many in Italian) and symbols that composers both old and new use to convey their specific intentions; if you encounter one you don't know, look it up. Wherever you see markings, it's always useful to ask: What does this mean? What does it tell me about the dramatic life of this particular moment?

8. **Musical form and use of motifs.** Are there certain musical elements that recur between phrases? Sections of the song that seem to repeat, such as

a refrain? When a musical motif is heard repeatedly in a song, it adds significance to the phrases where it appears. Are there occasions where material that's been introduced is transformed in some way? Transformations of musical or textual material create layers of meaning because we recall earlier occurrences of the theme or motif as we are hearing the transformed version. For example, consider the versions of "Can't Help Lovin' That Man" heard in the early and late scenes of *Show Boat*, or the reprise of "Prima Donna" in *Phantom of the Opera*.

With this checklist in mind, mark Δs in your study copy of the music over the beat just prior to the beginning of each new phrase. Dings should be precisely located on the music, because they occur at specifically designated moments within the organized time structure of the song. When you mark a ding in your music, you are giving yourself a visual reminder that what comes after the ding differs in some significant way from what precedes it.

When analyzing the musical score of your song, it's helpful to have a grasp on basic music skills, and most reputable BFA training programs seek to equip singing actors with the skills necessary. You needn't be a composer to analyze a song any more than you need to be a lyricist to sing the words of a song, but it makes a big difference when you can understand the fundamentals of music well enough to recognize what the composer of your song is doing.

Creating "Turn-By-Turn" Directions

"How do you get to Carnegie Hall?"

It's an old joke. A lost out-of-towner approaches a musician on the streets of New York, asking for directions. The musician, misinterpreting the question, replies, "Practice, practice, practice."

Nowadays, though, the answer to that question might be something like this:

Get on I-95 N from Dickinson St and S Christopher Columbus Blvd

12 min (2.4 mi)

↑ 1. Head north on S 13th St toward Morris St

0.2 mi

➡ 2. Turn right at the 3rd cross street onto Dickinson St

1.0 mi

↰ 3. Turn left onto S Front St

0.3 mi

➡ 4. Turn right onto Washington Ave

0.1 mi

↰ 5. Turn left onto S Christopher Columbus Blvd

0.4 mi

↰ 6. Turn left

125 ft

⅄ 7. Take the ramp to Interstate 676/Interstate 76/Central Phila

0.3 mi

Follow I-95 N to Dyer Ave in Manhattan, New York. Take the exit toward 42 Street/Uptown/Theater District/NY-9A from NY-495 E

1 h 29 min (94.3 mi)

⅄ 8. Merge onto I-95 N

18.2 mi

↰ 9. Keep left to stay on I-95 N

1.0 mi

⅄ 10. Keep right at the fork to stay on I-95 N, follow signs for Interstate 95 N
⚠ Partial toll road
ⓘ Entering New Jersey

9.2 mi

⅄ 11. Keep left at the fork and merge onto I-95
⚠ Partial toll road

54.6 mi

↑ 12. Continue straight onto I-95 N
⚠ Partial toll road

6.7 mi

↗ 13. Take exit 16E toward Lincoln Tunnel

0.6 mi

↑ 14. Continue onto NJ-495 E
⚠ Partial toll road

2.2 mi

↱ 15. Keep right to stay on NJ-495 E
⚠ Toll road
ℹ Entering New York

0.8 mi

↑ 16. Continue onto NY-495 E
⚠ Toll road

0.8 mi

⬉ 17. Take the exit on the left toward 42
Street/Uptown/Theater District/NY-9A
⚠ Partial toll road

390 ft

Take 10th Ave to W 57th St

9 min (1.5 mi)

↑ 18. Continue onto Dyer Ave

417 ft

↰ 19. Turn left onto W 41st St

486 ft

↱ 20. Turn right at the 1st cross street onto 10th Ave
ℹ Pass by CVS Photo (on the left)

0.8 mi

↱ 21. Turn right onto W 57th St
ℹ Pass by Duane Reade (on the right in 0.4 mi)
ℹ Destination will be on the right

0.5 mi

Carnegie Hall
881 7th Ave, New York, NY 10019

That's right, these are turn-by-turn directions from my front door to Carnegie Hall. These 21 steps will get you reliably from South Philly to 881 Seventh Avenue in New York.

"The trip to Carnegie Hall" sounds like a single thing, defined by a destination and the concerted effort it takes to get there. However, completing that trip requires numerous specific, detailed steps that must be executed in the right sequence and at the right time. Turn too soon or too late, miss a turn, turn in the wrong direction, and you're screwed. Execute all 21 steps, though, each one at the correct moment, and you can count on arriving at your destination. (Parking is, of course, a whole other challenge.)

Turn-by-turn directions help to reduce the stress of traveling. When they are available, I don't have to worry about every single thing at once or memorize my entire trip, I just have to continue in the direction I'm heading until it's time to execute the next turn. As I approach a turn, I become more alert, knowing that turning is likely to be a little more challenging than going straight. I might decide to slow down, look around, check the traffic and the landscape. When it's time, I execute the required maneuver, and then it's done. Now I'm on a new road, and I can relax, knowing there isn't much to do except enjoy the road until I get to the next turn.

In a similar way, musical theater educators often use the metaphor of "the journey of the song" to describe the events that occur in between a song's first notes and its final double bar. The character singing sets out with a destination in mind, but in between the point of departure and the final destination, many different events occur, and the words, notes, thoughts and feelings of the song are propelled by the momentum of the musical accompaniment.

This is why I'm such an enthusiastic proponent of breaking your song down into phrases. The dings in your song, the moments where each new phrase begins, are like the individual events in a list of turn-by-turn directions. The dings are the moments when you need to make a turn; in between the dings, you can proceed with confidence and ease until you approach the next one.

Marking up your music with dings and examining the unique features of each phrase is therefore a crucial way to fashion "turn-by-turn" directions for your performance.

Once you've transcribed your lyric, reformat it and rearrange it on the page if you need to and then get busy marking up that sucker. Add action verbs, adjectives, inner monologue, commentary and anything else that you find helpful, anything that will add richness and texture and specificity to your behavioral choices. When will you breathe? Pause? Add an accent or hold a word out for emphasis? When does the music slow down or speed up? With so many different kinds of choices to make–face, focus, gesture, movement, voice, breath, music, subtext and intention–marking up your secret copy is an invaluable way to remember and commit to the behavioral choices you've made. It's an essential part of the crafting process for serious singing-acting.

Later, in Chapter 15, I'll show you two tools you can use to facilitate this process: a SAVI Beat Sheet designed to collect and organize useful information, and a procedure for making a 4x6 index card for each phrase, with annotations and images to support imaginative choice-making. The cards will serve as a physical embodiment of the individual phrases of the song, a series of events arranged according to the principle of *"E pluribus unum,"* a singularity with multiple parts.

From Analysis to Synthesis, With SAVI Cards

Once you're clear on *where* the dings occur and *why* they occur in your piece, practice using one-two focus shifts at each ding, matching your gaze to the phrase until you feel confident about your able to coordinate the movement of your eyes with the beginning of each new phrase. Record yourself doing these focus shifts with the camera in your phone or laptop, then watch the playback and see whether you've got the hang of it.

Now you're ready to add some behavior ideas from your SAVI Cards. This part of the work should feel much like what you did with the content-neutral songs in the previous section of the workbook; that is, you'll choose and use one card per phrase. Work on your song one section at a time, choosing enough cards so that you have one for each phrase in the section. Choose cards from a variety of categories: a few faces, a few adjectives, a few gestures (body, face, partner, space), a few other adjustments. If you've got an idea for a choice, write it on a blank Custom Card and put it into the sequence.

Lay the cards out in sequence to match the phrases of the song, and practice incorporating the prompt on each card immediately after the One-Two focus shift. Pay attention to which cards work well and which ones don't; replace the ones that aren't working with other options from the deck and try again. Remember, sometimes it's helpful to start by settling on a choice for the last phrase, then deciding on a choice for the next-to-last phrase, and building your sequence backwards from the last moment to the first. Use the camera for feedback if you need an objective eye.

I recommend building each section in this manner and then linking the sections together to create a performance of the entire song. This deliberate and methodical procedure is an effective way to prepare repertoire for performance by exploring a variety of behavior options for a song. Your goal is to decide on the sequence that works best so that you can finalize those choices and commit yourself to executing them fully in performance. This is what I mean when I talk about "crafting" a performance. It's very similar to the procedure a songwriter uses when they construct a song.

When you've got a sequence you like, you can save it by writing it down in your notes or on the working copy of your sheet music. You can also put the related SAVI Cards into a plastic organizer page (like the ones used for storing trading cards.) That way, you can preserve the cards in the order you like best, and you can even review your sequence silently as an effective "brush-up rehearsal" before a performance.

Summary of Rep Prep Procedure

- Print out two copies of your song, one marked for the accompanist, the other for you to mark up with your dings and behavioral choices.
- Identify the dramatic event of the song by asking Stanislavski's fundamental questions, examining the text closely, and studying the musical it comes from if you have access to it.
- Type the lyrics of your song into the computer and format them so that each phrase is on a separate line, using the guidelines provided to determine where one phrase ends and the next one begins.
- Practice using one-two focus shifts at each ding.
- Select some of your SAVI Cards from an assortment of categories and begin to explore the choices you want to make. Use one card per phrase, changing cards with each focus shift.
- Try different variations on the sequence, swapping ideas and cards in and out, allowing yourself to inhabit each choice until you find a sequence you think works well for the song.
- Memorize the sequence and practice executing your choices in order from memory.
- Store the cards in an organizer sheet to keep them in order and so that you can review your sequence as part of your final preparations for performance.

Though it may seem tedious at first, be patient and thorough with this work. As soprano Beverly Sills was fond of pointing out, "There are no shortcuts to any place worth going."[37]

---

[37] Quoted in John Mason's *Conquering an Enemy Called Average* (Tulsa, Insight International, 2015).

CHAPTER 14

"Max A" (Maximizing Your Authenticity)

The legendary musical theater director George Abbott, famous for his no-nonsense manner, didn't hesitate to give actors line readings. "Do that but do it real," he'd say, without any further explanation of how to "do it real." To maximize your authenticity onstage, you need to know how bring "the realness" to your performance, but as you strive to do so, you'll be challenged by the slipperiness of the term "authentic" as well as the diversity of the musical theater repertoire. Often, the word "authentic" is used to mean "natural"; that is, unconstrained by arbitrary rules or customs and free from the usual BS. Trouble is, there's nothing "natural" about expressing oneself in song.

When it comes to the performing arts, authenticity is therefore a bit of a paradox. It's the mysterious force that brings the breath of life to something as artificial as a plié or as technical as a C major scale. In your quest for Maximum SAVI, you'll want to use the "Magic If" (p. 29) and the "First Heartbeat" (p. 112) techniques I described earlier to get you moving in the right direction. This chapter offers several other proven methods for achieving "Max A," including speaking the text, paraphrasing, personalization, and imaginary partner work.

Speaking the Text

The first tool you should use in your quest for maximum authenticity is a simple one: speak the lyric of your song as a monologue. This is a tool some directors wisely use when rehearsing a musical. They ask the actors to speak the text of their songs before singing them in order to draw attention to the meaning of the words and the primacy of communication in their delivery. To get the fullest value from this experience, speak the words not in the singsong way you might speak a poem, but with a strong commitment to their meaning and the truth they grow out of.

When you first begin to explore a song lyric as spoken text, ignore the music entirely and disregard how the rhythms in the musical score dictate the timing of your delivery. Instead, look for the words in the text that have significance and force, and try to bring out those values in your speaking. Bring onomatopoeia to the words in the text, especially the keywords, using timbre, diction, rhythm, pitch and inflection to express the essence of the words.

After you've spent some time in the practice room or the rehearsal room speaking the text without regard for the music, try to gradually reintroduce the rhythms of the song. Emphasize the syllables in your spoken delivery that are accented in the music. Pause your speaking when a rest occurs in the music; match the pace the composer has given you for the delivery of the words in the rhythms of the song. Consider the choices you might make regarding the rhythmic delivery of your song. Sometimes you have to execute the written rhythms exactly, especially in ensemble singing, but sometimes you can "loosen up" the rhythms slightly so that your delivery has more of a speechlike quality.

In the next step of your exploration, gradually bring the pitches of the song back into your delivery. Try speaking in a way that follows the contour of the melody without actually matching every written pitch; when the pitches in the melody get higher, raise the pitch of your speaking voice without actually worrying about singing the exact notes. Have the accompanist play your song while you deliver the spoken text in an approximation of the music. By the time you're through, you want to have explored the "middle ground" between natural speech and song as thoroughly as possible.

If you want to try out these procedures, turn back to Chapter 12 and speak the lyric of "I'll Be Known."

Paraphrase

One of the most powerful tools I know for song preparation is the **paraphrase**: restating the lyrics of a song in your own words. It's one of the best places to start when you're working on a song, and it's an exercise to return to when you're looking for ways to make your interpretation more specific and more personal.

Paraphrase is a terrific demonstration of the idea of inter-pretation as authorship. Putting the lyricist's words into your own gives you a greater sense of ownership of those words. It is entirely understandable to feel awkward as you begin to paraphrase. Most of the stuff you say when you paraphrase *ad lib* sounds pretty crappy, especially when you're extemporizing and the orig-inal lyric you're working with is a good one. The task you've been given is not to create great literature, but rather to dig deeper into the messy heart of the lyric. Say yes to the mess.

Paraphrase may be a brilliant exercise that integrates anal-ysis and synthesis, but it's only useful when you work phrase by phrase. A vague approximation of the overall feeling of the song gets boring very quickly, even as it's coming out of your mouth. Instead, you must dig deeply into the meaning of each individual phrase, with particular attention paid to personaliza-tion. Afterward, you must put that meaning together with vocabu-lary and feeling that is authentic and expressive.

There are several different ways that paraphrasing can be useful, depending on the type of lyric with which you're working. Some lyrics are pithy and compact, and in such cases, the para-phrase can help you to find additional richness and nuance in its very brief statements. If you're working on a song with phrases of just a few syllables (a common experience), paraphrase is a tool that can guide you toward a deeper and more expansive sense of the meaning of the phrase.

In my earlier specimen song, "I'll Be Known," Mary makes simple direct statements like "I want to be heard/I want to be seen." If I were an actress paraphrasing that stanza of the song, I might use language like, "Everyone always tells me I should shut up, but I'm so sick and tired of that! I feel like I'm invisible. People walk past me and it's like I'm not even there!" In this type of paraphrase, adding language can add richness and emotional resonance to lines that are otherwise rather spare.

On the other hand, some lyrics are elaborate and flowery. This is the case with *The Pirates of Penzance*, in which the celebrated lyricist W. S. Gilbert (technically not a relation, though I consider him a sort of spiritual great-great-grandfather) often builds his songs out of long, gracefully embroidered lines of verse. In such cases, a well-crafted paraphrase can help you discern the heart of a text and express it in a way that has greater impact for you.

> Oh, is there not one maiden breast
> That does not feel the moral beauty
> Of making worldly interest
> Subordinate to sense of duty?

You could paraphrase this stanza by saying, "Isn't there any girl willing to love me? Someone who knows that duty is more important than selfish pleasures?" Of course, the elegant rhetorical construction in Gilbert's lyrics gets lost in this paraphrase, but the language of the paraphrase is more direct and "actable" than the more poetic original.

When you craft a paraphrase, you're seeking words that capture the spirit and the attitude of the lyric as well as its content. That means it's worth spending time and effort to craft a good one. Extemporizing is a fine way to start working on a paraphrase, but finding the best words will take some trial and error. Once you find the right words, they're worth saving for future use. Try paraphrasing first with a pencil and paper, but speak the phrases aloud, with emotion and commitment, and you'll quickly see if you've found words that work or if you need to keep searching.

Is there a difference between paraphrase and subtext? Yes, although they are certainly related. **Subtext** is the term Stanislavski coined to describe the unspoken thoughts, feelings and motivations that are in the character's mind during any given moment in the drama of a play. Often these thoughts and feelings exist at the subverbal level, which is to say that they are so inchoate that they have not been channeled and formed in language.

When subtext is verbalized, it takes the form of inner monologue. Subtext and inner monologue are a private affair, existing only in the mind and private thoughts of the character. They give rise to the text of the scene, the words that the character chooses to say as a result of his thoughts and feelings. Meanwhile, paraphrase is a way of restating the text in more personalized language. Constructing an effective paraphrase involves exploring the subtext and inner monologue of the character; that is, using analysis and imagination to arrive at a very specific understanding of what's going on inside the character. Crafting the paraphrase involves using that understanding to restate the text of the song in new language.

Personalization

In a recent Broadway revival of the musical *Carousel*, Joshua Henry played the role of Billy Bigelow, and his work as an actor was heaped with critical praise.[38] At the end of the first act, Billy sings the famous "Soliloquy," a song prompted by the news that his wife, Julie, is pregnant and that he will soon be a father. As it turns out, Henry's real-life wife Cathryn was pregnant with their first child during the rehearsals and previews of that production.

[38] Laura Collins-Hughes, "Joshua Henry Does Whatever It Takes, in 'Carousel' and as a Father," *New York Times,* May 10, 2018, www.nytimes. com/2018/05/10/ theater/joshua-henry-carousel-billy-bigelow.html.

In Billy Bigelow's "Soliloquy," he wrestles with his feelings and reactions and shares them with the audience, who function as a trusted confidante. The dramatic event of the song begins not with the first sung words, but rather with the introductory, instrumental **vamp,** or extemporization. That introduction is one of the most important opportunities the song provides the actor to create behavior. Before a word is uttered, the audience is looking for some sign of what's going on in Billy's thoughts. Facial expression, body language and gesture can say a great deal at this moment, and even Billy's eyes can be expressive, communicating via "eye language."

When Joshua Henry poured out his heart about "my little girl" in the song "Soliloquy," he was able to use personalization to achieve an exceptional degree of authenticity. We're not all so fortunate as to have our present life circumstances provide such powerful emotional raw material for our stage performances, but this particular example dramatizes the power that personalization can provide in your pursuit of greater personal truth in your work on the stage.

Once you've answered Stanislavski's fundamental questions and studied the dramatic event of the song, ask yourself, *What aspects of my own life experience are similar to the dramatic circumstances of this song? Have I felt the feelings expressed in this song?* This sort of personal inquiry is meant to help you behave "as if" the given imaginary circumstances of the dramatic event of the song were really true.

Personalization can also be used to endow your partner, whether real or imaginary, and your relationships in a song or scene with greater truth. Ask yourself, *Is there someone in my life with whom I have a relationship comparable to the one I have with my partner in this scene? Have I had a romantic partner like the individual to whom I sing this love song? A friend and trusted confidante I can "substitute" and cast in the role of the imaginary confidante to whom I sing this confession? An experience I've had that affected me in the way that I am affected by the dramatic event of this song?*

Go ahead, give it a try! Pick a song that you're working on and test out the power of personalization.

The Imaginary Partner

To take your authenticity to the next level, one great tool is to approach a solo song "as if" it were a scene, with either a real or an imaginary partner. The singing actor spends an inordinate amount of time alone onstage, standing solo in front of a class or an audience, lacking the kind of provocation that brings a scene to life. An experience involving another actor as a scene partner or provocateur can be a very useful tool for discovering the dramatic event of a solo song more fully. This can be either improvised or prepared in advance; both options add value to your performance. For instance, if you're singing a song to your imagined beloved, find someone willing to pretend to be the object of your affections and sing the song to them. Better still, give them free rein to respond to what you're singing and doing to them, and then respond to their reactions as you sing.

Scene partners for songs come in all shapes and sizes, but I've found there are a few types that are especially useful:

The Confidante. This sort of imaginary partner is someone you feel comfortable sharing your most private secrets with. You're willing to confess your hopes, your fears and your dreams to a trusted confidante. When you're excited, you can't wait to share that excitement with them. When you're feeling down, you feel certain that your confidante will sympathize and maybe even help you figure out what to do to make things better. Many musical theater solo songs are sung to a confidante, and while there are plenty of occasions in which that confidante shares the stage with the singer, it's frequently the case that the confidante exists only in the singer's mind. Examples of songs sung to an imaginary confidante include "Will He Like Me?", "Tonight at Eight," and the title song from *She Loves Me*.

The Antagonist. This imaginary partner is your opponent, someone who's out to do you in. Of course, the great thing about an imaginary antagonist is that you can make him sit still while you heap him with verbal abuse. Singing a song to an imaginary antagonist lets you vent your feelings of frustration and anger. Lots and lots of musical theater songs include a real-life antagonist, but examples of songs sung to an imaginary antagonist include "Shall I Tell You What I Think of You?" from *The King and I* and "Just You Wait" from *My Fair Lady*.

The Object. In grammar, a transitive verb has an object, a word describing the person or entity affected by the action of the verb. For instance, in the sentence "The teacher instructed her pupil," "her pupil" is the object. In many musical theater songs, you are seeking to persuade or influence someone who can be described as the *object* of that action. There are, of course, all sorts of reasons why you might want to persuade or influence someone, and all sorts of ways to do it, but musical theater songs often present an act of persuasion, which requires an object. Examples include Mama Rose's desperate effort to persuade her daughter Louise in the song "Everything's Comin' Up Roses" at the end of the first act of *Gypsy*, and Professor Harold Hill persuading the citizens of River City that the arrival of a new pool table in town means "Trouble" in *The Music Man*.

An imaginary partner is not merely a passive target or someone for you to act upon. The best imaginary partners are responsive, answering you back with some sort of question or retort at just the right moment to prompt you to sing the next phrase in your song. Those responses are often quite simple: "What do you mean?", "I don't believe you!", "I don't understand."

When examining a solo song, resist the temptation to say, "I'm just thinking out loud" or "I'm singing to myself." These choices almost never serve you well. See if you can't find a way to reframe your song as a conversation with a confidante, an antagonist, or an object of some kind.

Summary

Maximizing your authenticity should always be one of your goals as a singing actor. In this chapter, I've shared some of my best ideas for how to make that happen:

- Defining the dramatic event in a way that's meaningful and personal;
- Speaking the text without the music to get more intimately in familiar with the essence of what you're saying;
- Paraphrasing the text to put the author's words into your own words;
- Personalizing the drama by looking for examples from your own experience that are analogous to the ones depicted in the drama;
- Defining your solo song as a scene with an imaginary partner, either a confidante, an antagonist or an object.

Optimal realness awaits you when you apply these techniques to the song of your choice!

CHAPTER 15

"Max V" (Maximizing your Variety)

If you've been resourceful and diligent in your pursuit of maximum specificity, then you're already well on your way to Max V. Greater variety is almost invariably the result when you become super-specific about each individual phrase and the dings that separate them in a song.

In this chapter, though, I want to consider the challenges you will face when dealing with multiple phrases. We'll look at phrases in pairs, examining the most common types of dings you will encounter. We'll consider how phrases can sometimes be linked or arranged into sets or groups, and what this means for you as a performer. I'll also offer strategies for avoiding some of the common mistakes that diminish variety. I want to help you optimize your ability to differentiate phrases and make clear changes at each transitional moment so that you can attain Max V.

The Taxonomy of Dings

Why are transitions or dings so important when you sing? A ding is a moment of change, and change means contrast. When the listener is presented with two consecutive phrases, the second of which differs in some verbal, musical or behavioral way, the mind of the listener is engaged in making sense of that difference (even though they may not realize it).

The so-called **contrast principle** is fundamental to how we make sense of information or sensory input. A statement will have greater impact when it is presented in a way that accentuates its contrast from the previous one. For example, the statement "I weigh 185 pounds" becomes more meaningful when I also say, "I used to weigh 220 pounds." If, instead, I precede that same statement with different information–"I used to weigh 150 pounds"–the statement means something quite different. We experience pleasure more fully when it's preceded by pain, and a room seems brighter when we emerge from darkness. It is axiomatic that "contrast operates within, and often amplifies, every aspect of persuasion,"[39] and persuasion, the art of influencing others, is just another word for what characters in a dramatic event do when they sing with intention.

When the principle **"Contrast creates meaning"** is applied to song analysis, it shows why it is important for us to focus on what makes each phrase *different* from its predecessor, and how that difference serves to create meaning. When analyzing a lyric, ask yourself, *In what ways is this phrase **different from** the one that precedes it? Are there ways in which it is the **same as** the one that precedes it? What can I discern about the thought process of the character who's singing by understanding that difference?*

Often, those changes will be apparent from the language in the phrases. There are also potentially meaningful things you may discover when you compare two phrases musically and structurally. The following are some comparative questions you might ask to gain this insight:

- Which phrase is longer (has more syllables)?
- Which is shorter (has fewer syllables)?
- Higher in pitch? Lower?
- Is there a contrast in the phrases' melodic contour?
- Are there adjustments to interval size?
- Adjustments to rhythm? Words of longer duration? Shorter?

[39] Robert Cialdini, quoted in Daniel H. Pink, *To Sell is Human: The Surprising Truth about Moving Others* (New York: Penguin, 2012).

- Do these structural differences provide any clues regarding changes in content?

Phrases in Groups

As you begin to consider phrases in relationship to one another, it soon becomes apparent that certain phrases are meant to be understood as part of a group. When phrases are grouped together, the meaning emerges not just from the individual phrase but from the way it functions in its group. Phrases can be grouped in pairs, in larger sets or even in lists. I've made a list of some common groupings below.

Linked phrases: one or more than one? Sometimes a single phrase conjoins two or more contrasting concepts in a way that makes it tricky to discern whether you're dealing with a single phrase or several different phrases.

In certain lyrics, meaning is to be found in the ***juxtaposition*** (in Latin, literally the "placing next to") of two contrasting consecutive phrases rather than in the content of one specific phrase or the other. The Gershwin's song "Let's Call The Whole Thing Off" is a good demonstration of this principle at work; the meaning of the song is not that someone says "ee-ther" or that someone says "eye-ther," but rather that two people have different pronunciations of the same word.

The title of one of the songs from Stephen Sondheim's *Company* further illustrates this point: "Sorry-Grateful." The full meaning of this lyric is created in the tension between the different meanings of the two words in the title. How can one be sorry and grateful at the same time? Can a relationship that contains both sorrow and gratitude be a good thing? Sondheim explores the state of ambivalence in many song lyrics like this. For the singer to not make an adjustment of some kind in between the first phrases (acknowledging that "grateful" is something quite different than "sorry") would deprive the lyric of its meaning entirely. And yet, singers do. They get seduced by the lovely ballad music and the sound of their own voice and fail to deliver the content.

In considering whether linked phrases should be treated separately or as a single unit, it's useful to ask: Is the journey of the song leading the singer from one thought or point of view to an opposing point of view? Or is the singer holding both opposing points of view in his or her mind, completely aware of the tension their opposition creates? Is he or she assessing or considering options or alternatives? If so, is this happening sequentially, one option at a time, or are the options simultaneously present in the mind of the singer? The distinguishing answers to these questions are important to understanding the journey of the song.

As an exercise, try creating a pair of sung gibberish phrases that are linked, and explore how sound and behavior can work together to create a sense of meaning. Or work with a content-neutral song like "The ABC Song" and make it into conjoined pairs:

△ (Consider this statement) A B C D E F G
△ (But then consider the opposite) H I J K L M N O P
△ (On the one hand) Q R S
△ (But then on the other hand) T U V

What kinds of behavioral choices seem most useful when dealing with a pair of linked phrases? A little experimentation soon makes it clear that shifts of focus and other simple behavioral adjustments are key to delineating the contrasts between items in a linked pair or set.

Lists. Lists are a common occurrence in many musical theater songs, and require some special consideration. A list is an extended set of linked phrases, in which all the individual phrases relate to some common purpose. They are the same (all part of the same category) but different, and it is important to be especially clear on what makes them different.

William S. Gilbert, Cole Porter, and Stephen Sondheim are among the masters of the "list song" or "catalog song." W. S. Gilbert's famous patter song "I Am the Very Model of a Modern Major-General" is an excellent example of a list. In it, Major General Stanley lists all the things he's good at, in a virtuoso display of tongue-twisting elocution. A key to a successful performance of that song is the ability to differentiate the items on the list while maintaining the breathless rat-a-tat delivery the song requires. Cole Porter has given us many memorable list songs like "You're the Top." A more modern-day example of a list song would be "Could I Leave You?" from Sondheim's *Follies*, in which an angry wife lists all the things she'd be giving up if she divorced her husband. In all these cases, it's crucially important that the singer have specific imagery in mind and use specific behavior to differentiate the items on the list. In addition, you must discover within the scene the impulses that cause you to continue to add to your list.

Refrains and text that repeats. Songs are often built of phrases or stanzas that repeat. Perhaps the most common example is the strophic song with a recurring refrain, like "Sit Down, You're Rockin' The Boat" from *Guys and Dolls*. Such songs are constructed of a series of **strophes** (two or more lines repeated as a unit) or stanzas alternating with a refrain that is identical each time. Similar to this is a song form where the final line of each stanza is the same, like "I Hate Men" from *Kiss Me Kate,* in which each stanza actually both begins *and* ends with the title phrase.

As an exercise, build sequences of phrases that mimic this sort of song structure. Working as a group, create a phrase or short series of phrases made up of gibberish and behavior which will be designated as the "refrain." Then create an improvisation where each member of the circle invents a phrase or two in gibberish and behavior as their individual "verse," with the group singing the agreed-upon "refrain" in between each verse.

Meet the Ding Family!

I've spent a lot of time thinking about phrases and dings in songs, examining the different ways one phrase can lead to another. It turns out there's a fairly small number of ways in which a new phrase can relate to the phrase that preceded it.

"And" ("More")	The subsequent phrase is not just a continuation of the antecedent phrase but an elaboration or intensification of it. The character singing provides more detail and/or supporting example(s). A longer phrase with more syllables is a sign of elaboration. Changes in pitch produce intensification.
"I Mean" (Modification)	A slight modification of the previous phrase, using other words to communicate a more precise meaning.
"But"	Contradicting or significantly departing from the previous phrase, a major adjustment in the train of thought occurs or is made, revealing a (possibly concealed) truth.
"Aha"	A discovery or revelation, or a new insight has occurred to the character at the onset of the subsequent phrase.
"New"	"New" dings occur at the onset of a new(ish) idea or train of thought. In a "new" ding, the subsequent phrase has little relationship to the antecedent phrase. Sometimes the relationship between the antecedent phrase and the subsequent phrase can be random, or seemingly random.
"Back"	"Back" dings link back to something said earlier, citing evidence to make a point. The beginning of a refrain or the title phrase of a song often starts with a "back" ding.
"Detour" (Parenthetical)	A momentary departure from the present train of thought, undertaken with the intention of returning to the previous after a brief interruption. A detour may be a footnote or side note, commenting on or revealing a hitherto unseen aspect of the subject. It may be a pair, a nested set of "new" and "back" impulses.

"Up"	"Up" dings take the insight to a higher level of abstraction. Language ascends out of the vernacular and may reference the title of the song.
"Down"	This ding gets down to brass tacks, down to business, no more messing around. It may go deeper, into greater depth, or become plainer, with more penetrating language.

This "taxonomy of dings" will seem abstract at first, but once you find examples of these types of transitions in songs, the categories will start to make much more sense and you'll soon realize they are a great way to take your analysis of song lyrics to new levels of insight. When you're analyzing a song, you will find it advantageous to use these categories to jumpstart your thinking about the transitions. In fact, it's a relief to have a concise set of specific options to choose from rather than an unlimited universe of possibilities. Use these categories as you fill out your SAVI Beat Sheet or make individual index cards for the phrases in your song, as described below.

Beat Sheet Instructions

I've created two different tools you can use for managing the information that emerges from the work of identifying types of dings and phrase groups. The first, called the SAVI Beat Sheet, appears below:[40] .

---

[40] There's a downloadable PDF of this worksheet on the Book Extras page of the website which will make it easy for you to print out copies.

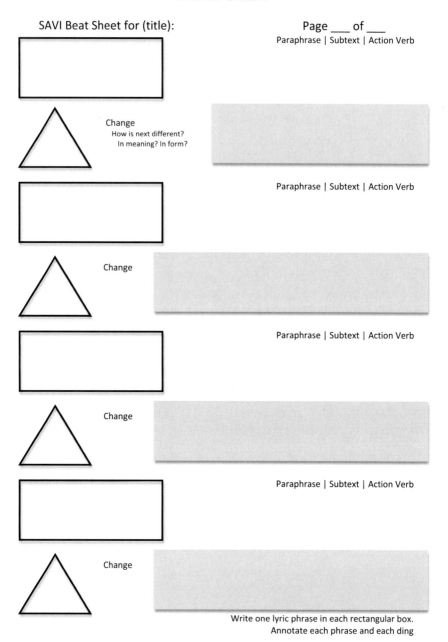

SAVI Beat Sheet for (title):

Page ___ of ___

Paraphrase | Subtext | Action Verb

Change
How is next different?
In meaning? In form?

Paraphrase | Subtext | Action Verb

Change

Paraphrase | Subtext | Action Verb

Change

Paraphrase | Subtext | Action Verb

Change

Write one lyric phrase in each rectangular box.
Annotate each phrase and each ding

Once you've divided the song up into phrases, copy the phrases into the rectangular boxes on the left side of the sheet, one phrase per box. The triangle below each rectangle represents the "ding" that separates the phrases, and is meant to be used as a place to describe how the next phrase (i.e., the one in the box below the triangle) differs from the current phrase (i.e., the one in the box above the triangle). The right side of the sheet is a place where you can make notes about paraphrase, subtext, and action.

Index Card Instructions

Using individual index cards, one per phrase, can help you go one step further in the work of dividing a song into phrases. For this step, you'll need either 3x5 or 4x6 index cards. Index cards that come on a ring work especially well for our purposes.

Divide the card in half by drawing a horizontal line midway down the card, then divide the bottom half again by drawing a vertical line in the middle of the card. Write the text of your phrase in the top half, using large printing that fills up the area and can be easily read from a couple feet away. If you're feeling artistic, make the handwriting or lettering you use reflect the emotional quality of the phrase itself: looping and lyrical, jagged and angry, bold and forceful. If a particular word seems especially important, use your artistic flair to decorate that word and make it look like what it means. And if there are words you don't know the meaning of, look them up in a dictionary! Nothing is worse than pretending you know what a word means (or what a proper name or slang term refers to) and trying to fudge it in performance.

In the lower left corner of your card, write a paraphrase of the text you've written in the top area; that is, restate the idea of the phrase using your own words, striving for vividness and immediacy. In the lower right hand corner, write an action verb in the infinitive form (e.g., to plead, to explain, to demand, to threaten). This will help you identify what it is that you are *doing* in this phrase of text. Pro tip: the action should be reflected in the paraphrase—-that is, let the "reality of doing" guide you as you reword the lyric.

There's probably an infinite number of ways to paraphrase the text of a song lyric, and a wide range of action verbs that you can choose. By writing them here, you're starting to commit to some performance choices, and in doing so, you're stepping up to the task of being the author of your performance. This is important, detailed work that is part of the preparation of any song, work that combines thoughtful analysis and creative synthesis. Give this work the time it deserves. Don't rush through and do a slapdash job! I suggest you do these in pencil because you'll probably continue to get new ideas about how to improve on these, and pencil will be easier to erase and edit later on.

The lowest right hand corner of the card is the place where you'll specify the transition from this card to the next. This will be easier to discern once you've written out both cards and examined them side by side. Choose one the types of dings from the chart above, adding whatever annotation you think might be useful.

Having prepared a half-dozen or so cards of your song, spread them out on a tabletop in a row. This is an opportunity for you to consider them as a **sequence**, a progression of thoughts in which you can discern a particular relationship between any pair or series of consecutive thoughts. This broader view gives you a perspective from which you can re-consider any of the dings you've chosen.

Here's a sample card, showing the layout I've described in the previous paragraphs.

The text of your phrase goes in the top half.

Write it big

Or small or pretty and style it to match

Define any unfamiliar vocabulary.
Are there proper names, terms or special words?

Paraphrase	**Action verb**
Use your own words	Use the infinitive: "to _____"
Choose language that feels vivid true to you and embodies your interpretative choices	
	Next Action/Transition
	What type of ding?
	"More," "I mean," "But," "Aha," "New," "Back," "Detour," "Up," "Down"

While you've got the phrase cards you've made laid out on the table, go through your SAVI Cards and choose one to go with each phrase. You can use cards from any category, and I encourage you to try out a variety of choices, including ones that might seem unconventional or not obviously suited to the phrase. Try out your choices by singing through the phrases while applying the behavior choices from your SAVI Cards; make a note of the ones you like best, swap out the ones that don't seem to serve you well, and keep exploring until you've got a sequence of SAVI Cards that seems to suit the progression of phrases in the lyric.

EXERCISE: Silent Rehearsal

A benefit of turning your song into a stack of index cards is that it gives you the ability to conduct what I call a "Silent Rehearsal."

In developing this technique, I was inspired by the fact that athletes and others recovering from injuries derive benefits from visualizing exercises even if they're unable to do them.[41] A silent

---

[41] Dryw Dworsky and Vikki Krane, "Using the Mind to Heal the Body: Imagery for Injury Rehabilitation," Association for Applied Sport Psychology, https://

rehearsal with your phrase cards will have a similar benefit for you because you will use the cards to lead yourself through a visualization of your performance.

Look at each card in sequence, reading the information on the card and visualizing the behaviors you will create during that phrase. Consciously arrange your facial muscles in a way that corresponds to the facial behavior you intend to create when you sing, and allow the information on the card to affect your breathing for a few seconds. After allowing enough time to pass for you to fully visualize the phrase and externalize it in your face and breath, move that card to the bottom of the pile (the ring will come in handy here) and go on to the next phrase. After working through the stack of cards without regard for time, try doing it while spending a period of time on each card equal to the amount of time it will take you to sing that phrase, or while listening to a recording of your song.

Try the silent rehearsal as preparation before you sing in class, as you wait in the hallway before an audition, or in the dressing room as you prepare for a show. It's remarkably productive and concrete for bringing maximum specificity ("Max S") and maximum variety ("Max V") to the performance you're about to give.

Don't "Go with the Flow"!

If your goal is to maximize the Variety of your singing-acting, one of the biggest mistakes you can make is to "go with the flow." Most songs, including theater songs, are organized around a steady beat, with musical accompaniment serving as a kind of conveyor belt that carries the lyric along. This is especially true in rock songs, but it's also true in ballads and jazzy songs, any song that has a steady groove.

I'm a strong proponent of learning how to fight the groove, to disrupt the steady flow of the music. Regardless of whether your song is a ballad or a "bop," even if the beat is steady and the accompaniment homogeneous, you must organize your behavior

appliedsportpsych.org/resources/injury-rehabilitation/using-the-mind-to-heal-the-body-imagery-for-injury-rehabilitation/.

choices in a way that highlights the beginning, middle and end of each phrase, letting the content of the lyric and the structure of the vocal melodies be your guide. The procedures I've introduced in this chapter will help you bring out the expressive details in any song, create greater meaning through stronger contrast, and navigate the journey of the song without being swept away by its musical current.

Shish kebab, not applesauce, right? You got this!

CHAPTER 16

"Max I" (Maximizing Your Intensity)

Intensity, the fourth fundamental attribute of effective singing-acting, is the quality that makes musical theater performers seem a little bit "extra." Of course, your work needs to be Specific, Authentic and Varied, but it also must be Intense to deliver the thrill audiences expect from a musical. As spectators, we yearn to see performers pushing against the boundaries of the possible, defying the limitations that constrain us ordinary mortals. The performer's pursuit of Maximum Intensity is a never-ending quest for *more*. It is the aspect of musical theater performance that is most like an athletic competition.

So, naturally, we'll begin our discussion of Maximum Intensity with by considering the importance of ease.

Excuse me?

Finding Ease in the Critical Moments

Really, it's not that counter-intuitive. The most effective thing we can do in your pursuit of Maximum Intensity is to make the most of the capacity we already have, and that involves eliminating unwanted tension that serves to constrain us as we go all out.

Alexander Technique teachers use the term **critical moment** to describe any moment of "crisis," any turning point where your future outcome will be determined by the choices you make in the present moment. Often, those moments of crisis are accompanied by high levels of intensity: Elphaba's song "Defying Gravity" at the end of Act I of *Wicked*, for instance, or Valjean's decision to reveal himself ("2-4-6-0-1!") in the cart scene of *Les Mis*. In such moments, the performer's nervous system shifts into "fight-or-flight" mode, whether we mean to or not. The stressful emotions of the moment trigger the release of cortisol and other hormones that activate the autonomic nervous system as it would if you were a caveman in the presence of a saber-tooth tiger.

What role does ease play in these critical moments? Let me answer that question with another question: if you wanted to drive your car as fast as possible, would you put on the emergency brake? If you wanted to jump as high as you could, would you wear heavy boots? Success in the critical moment requires intense effort coordinated with an optimal sense of ease, so that you can get the maximum possible benefit from that effort. This requires you to learn to cast aside the encumbrance of unnecessary habitual tensions and inefficient self-use.

Any moment that occurs right before you begin to do something you consider a challenge will be a "critical moment." As you prepare to do something stressful, your limbic system triggers the production of cortisol, causing the body to brace itself unconsciously, almost reflexively; the neck and spine contract slightly, the joints stiffen and your sensory awareness decreases. For singing actors, this moment can occur as you begin to sing a song–the moment when you make the transition from "not performing" to "performing"–or at any moment when the singing gets particularly loud or high or tricky. At that critical moment, you think to yourself "get ready, get set, go," but as you "get set," you lose the freedom that is essential to beginning your activity with ease and poise. You think, "I'm going to bear down, try harder, make more of an effort," all in the name of achieving success, but all these thoughts, and the subconscious neurological and physiological changes that accompany them, diminish your chances of achieving the very success you seek.

I have found it very helpful to think of the beginning of each new phrase or ding as a kind of critical moment in the journey of the song. As you finish doing one thing (singing a phrase, playing an action) and prepare to do the next thing, there is a tendency to hold over the effort and tension associated with the previous phrase. I have a colleague who describes this using the analogy of playing the piano: muscles are like piano keys that must be released before you can press them again. There is much to be gained by thinking of each new phrase as a new event, and for the

SAVI singing actor who seeks to work phrase by phrase, the onset or beginning of each new phrase is a critical moment.

The study of Alexander Technique is designed to impart a sense of ease at those critical moments. You come to learn that you have a choice, and learn to inhibit or adjust the unconscious habits that interfere with your ability to make the optimal choice at that critical moment.

How, then, can one attain ease at the critical moment? As discussed in Chapter 11, one powerful strategy I have found to be effective is to "come to your senses." Effort causes you to not notice yourself. Asking the student to notice something, to attend to the quality of himself, is an effective way of reducing tension, according to one of my eloquent colleagues. As you approach the critical moment, allow yourself to take in as much sensory information as you can, not only from your body, but also from your companions (your partners in a scene, for instance) and your environment. When we sing, we are transmitting information, sending it out to be seen and heard by others, but you will experience greater ease if you allow yourself to *receive as well as transmit*. The moment when you take a breath, allow yourself to also take in information.

Alexander Technique teaches us that *how* we begin something is enormously important to how we will do what we've begun. This is true whether you're talking about getting up from a chair, climbing a step, or taking a breath to begin to sing a phrase. The moment just before we begin–that instant of "onset" when we make the transition from the previous thing to the impending next thing–is critical to the qualities we will bring to it.

Intensity Exercises and Études

In addition to finding ease in each transitional moment, achieving "Max I" requires that you learn to explore increasingly higher levels of intensity as well as to understand the difference between types of intensity and what they contribute to a dramatic event. The following exercises—the "Three-Peat" and the Laban Variations—will contribute positively to your success in these areas.

EXERCISE: The "Three-Peat"

Repetition is a valuable technique for attaining higher levels of intensity. Having just done something, if you do it *again* with the intention of giving a little bit more, going a little bit faster or making your behavior a little bit bigger, you'll find yourself reaching extremes you didn't initially think yourself capable of. This is the essential principle behind the "Three-Peat" (also known as the Echo Circle), an exercise that uses repetition in a call-and-response pattern. To begin, the members of your group should stand in a circle.

Level 1. One member of the group makes a sound, and the others echo it. The next person in the circle makes a sound, and the group echoes that. This repeats until everyone in the circle has been the leader.

Level 2. Beginning like Level 1, one member of the group makes a sound, and the others echo it. Now the person who first made the sound makes it again; the repeat can be an exact repetition, an intensification of the first sound, or an elaboration or embellishment of the first sound. The group echoes this sound. The leader now makes the sound a third time, choosing again from the options of repetition, intensification, or embellishment, and the group repeats that sound. Now the "lead" passes to the next person in the circle. A note for teachers on this level and those that follow: it's interesting to side-coach the leader to think of the second sound as being in some way a response to the group.

Level 3. Same as Level 2, but with a movement to go with the sound.

Level 4. Same, but with a short phrase of melody, using vowel sounds, gibberish, or some specified word or phrase (e.g., "sing your name"). Coaching note: as the call-and-response pattern moves back and forth between the soloist and the group, encourage the group to use their echo as an intensification or distortion of the leader's phrase. Ideally, the group should function so that the leader's phrase is multiplied by the number of voices in the room and the idea and the emotion of the phrase is enriched by the energy of the group. Then encourage the leader to try to pick up on that enhancement and incorporate some aspect of that into the next solo phrase.

Level 5. Same pattern, but each singer in the group should choose a phrase from a song they are working on. The leader should not only sing the phrase, but also create behavior (face, eyes, vocal tone, gesture, body language) that supports the phrase, and the group should copy and "multiply" the phrase. Each member of the group has the challenge of trying to sing the phrase exactly and of fully embodying the behavioral choices of the leader. Every member will have a slightly different take on the phrase, so the leader should be coached to watch and listen to the group to take in these variations, then distill them into the next repeat of the phrase.

Level 6. Use Garageband or a similar program to create a loop or drumbeat. Do the three-peats in time to the drumbeat. The phrases can be more like rock riffs in this variation, and can use any sort of text, including wordless sounds and rock-ish syllables like "Whoa-oa-oa" or "Hey-y-y-yeah!"

Three is an arbitrary number of repeats—-though let's face it, "The Four-Peat" doesn't sound nearly as cool. If you and your classmates are digging this sort of work, I encourage you to explore what happens when there are more repeats. Be sure to do "exact" repetitions, repetitions that develop intensity, and repetitions that develop or embellish the phrase.

With multiple repetitions, you can also go deeper into the truth of the phrase, making it an opportunity to link specificity and authenticity. Finally, as the work transitions from one leader to the next, you and your fellow participants get to experience a varied set of behaviors and "try on" each one with full commitment. It is, in short, a great exercise for developing maximum SAVI.

"More and More" (The Laban Variations)

The next exercise requires some introduction and a bit of background. Rudolf Laban, a choreographer, dancer and movement analyst from the first half of the twentieth century, spent much of his career developing an innovative set of tools for describing, notating and characterizing movement. He identified three particular qualities of movement-weight, speed (tempo or duration) and direction in the space (direction)-that helped to characterize a particular movement, and he invented dialectical pairs of descriptive adjectives associated with each of these qualities:

> Weight: Heavy (or "Strong") <----> Light
> Space: Direct <----> Indirect
> Time: Quick (or "Sudden") <----> Sustained

While Laban developed these descriptive pairs as a framework for describing different qualities of movement, I've come to associate vocal and musical meanings with them as well. The SAVI Cards include instructions that use Laban's terminology-"Heavier," "Lighter," "Quicker," "More Sustained," are part of the "Adjustments" category-so let's take a moment to explore their implications in the world of music and sound.

Heavier

△ ADJUSTMENTS

Quicker

△ ADJUSTMENTS

lighter

△ ADJUSTMENTS

more
sustained

△ ADJUSTMENTS

Describing voices as "Heavy" or "Light" refers not only to the quality or loudness of the sound but also to the muscular actions used to produce the sound.

Heavy	Light
Loud	Soft
Strong contraction of abdominal muscles during phonation	Little contraction of abs during phonation
Chest voice ("heavy mechanism")	Head voice ("light mechanism")
Dramatic ("playing the Heavy")	Lyric or comedic qualities

As an experiment, pick a vocal exercise you are familiar with or one of the études in this workbook and explore all the different ramifications of "heavy" and "light" sounds. Don't treat them as a binary proposition in which you must choose one or the other, but rather as two ends of a spectrum of possibilities. In other words, imagine a numerical scale where 10 is the heaviest and 1 is the lightest, and try singing with all the possibilities in between. At the same time, explore movements that have qualities of "heaviness" and "lightness" as you sing.

The complementary qualities of "Quick" and "Sustained" describe duration, and vocal sounds have duration as well.

Quick	Sustained
Fast tempo	Slow steady tempo
Short note durations ("staccato")	Full-value note durations ("tenuto")
Melodic line broken by silences	Notes smoothly connected together ("legato")

When vocalizing, it is productive to explore a range of "Quick" and "Sustained" qualities. As with the previous pair, think of them as a spectrum of possibilities rather than as an either/or binary. As you work on these musical qualities, explore movements that similarly employ a range of options between "Quick" and "Sustained."

"Direction" is the third of Laban's categories, and the music and vocal equivalencies for the two terms in this dialectical pair can be described thus:

Direct	Indirect
A simple melody with large note values and rhythms organized in regular patterns	A complicated melody with an irregular mix of short and long note values
Repeated notes	Large intervals and melodic leaps
A melody that moves in steps	An unsteady, irregular use of abdominal muscles during inhalation and exhalation
Steady, controlled use of the abdominal muscles in breath and phonation	

As with the first two pairs, it's good to practice and condition yourself using "Direct" and "Indirect" movement and vocal expression. Think about phrases in songs you know where a character expresses themselves directly ("I hate men!") or indirectly ("I got this really great gun/Shit, where is it?/No, it's really great/Wait/Shit, where is it?") and incorporate those qualities as you sing the variations of the étude "More and More."

Laban combined his three pairs in eight different ways to produce a comprehensive set of what he referred to as **effort actions:**

Press = Heavy + Direct + Sustained
Glide = Light + Direct + Sustained
Punch = Heavy + Direct + Quick
Dab = Light + Direct + Quick
Wring = Heavy + Indirect + Sustained
Float = Light + Indirect + Sustained
Slash = Heavy + Indirect + Quick
Flick = Light + Indirect + Quick

You'll find Laban's concepts are tremendously useful as you look for ways to explore and enrich the psycho-physical component of your performance. Working with Laban's effort actions compels you to be Specific in your choices, and to address issues of Intensity in your choices as well. (Can this choice have MORE weight? Be LESS sustained? MORE direct?) Moving from one effort action to another (a phrase of "Punch" followed by one of "Flick," for example) is a great way of building Variety. As you make a point of inhabiting each of your choices, you'll find that each one of the effort actions brings on certain kinds of feelings and communicates different sorts of emotions.

EXERCISE: More and More

"More and More" is an exercise that takes the musical form of a theme and variations. The basic theme, as you can see from the sheet music, is a pattern of ascending and descending thirds. As the accompaniment changes tempo, meter, mode and style, you will find the opportunity to move through all the effort actions in turn.

After you've sung a particular variation, sift through your SAVI Cards (particularly Emotions, Action Verbs, Adjectives and Gestures) to find ones that feel compatible with the music and vocality of that version. Then use those cards to develop performance choices that make your expression more specific and dramatic. You can also incorporate the six Icon Cards ("Heavier," "Lighter," "Quicker," "More Sustained," "More Direct" and "More Indirect") to suggest adjustments you can make to your choices along the way.

The first few times you sing the basic theme, sing it simply and evenly, with a neutral behavior state. Then slow down the tempo and increase your vocal weight to explore the qualities of the effort action "press": heavy, sustained and direct. As you sing, press the palms of your hands against a wall, or find a partner to push against. As you sing the words "more and more," try to intensify each of the three components of the effort action "press:" *more* heavy, *more* sustained, *more* direct. Which emotions seem to fit with the quality of "press?" Which actions? Which adjectives?

Variation I is marked *"martellato,"* which means "heavily accented and detached." This variation uses the effort action "punch." You should sing each syllable loudly, with great force, with a very short duration. Find movements that go with the quality of "punch"—using your hands and fists, of course, but other parts of your body as well. Take a very aggressive and direct attitude as you sing. Notice the different feeling you get as the sustained effort of "press" is replaced by the alacrity of "punch." Can you take a step with the quality of "punch?" Are there particular emotions, actions or adjectives that seem to fit especially well with the qualities of "punch"?

Variation II is marked "lightly," and uses the effort action "dab." Each syllable is short, but unlike "punch," it should be sung as lightly as possible. Gestures and movements should incorporate the qualities of "dab" as well: light, quick and direct. As you sing this variation, think about giving directions or instructions in a very calm and precise way. Can you make your voice and behavior lighter? Quicker? More direct? How does "dab" differ from "press" or "punch"? What emotions, action verbs and adjectives seem to correspond to the effort action "dab"?

Variation III is marked "Valse," and is written in three-quarter time, the time signature of the waltz. The effort action here is "glide," which is light and direct, like "dab," but sustained rather than quick. As you sing, glide across the floor to a partner or specific destination, or find a partner and waltz gracefully together.

Variation IV is marked "roughly," and uses the effort action "slash." In this variation, the sounds and movements are quick and forceful, but the movement is indirect rather than direct. Imagine that you are being menaced by opponents or demons approaching from all around you, and that you have to fend them off with a heavy sword. Does "slash" seem well suited to fear? To heroism? To passion? Which adjectives and action verbs in your deck fit well with "slash?"

Variation V is marked "agitato," which is the musical term that means "agitated." This phrase is meant to be sung with the effort action "flick," which is quick, light and indirect. "Flick" is similar to "dab" but not as controlled or focused. Think about brushing away a swarm of little bugs that are all around you, and use a panting breath in the rests between the words. This variation might be a good opportunity to explore comical behaviors.

Variation VI is marked "with anguish," and you'll note that this variation uses a minor scale. It is meant to be sung with the effort action "wring," which is heavy, sustained and indirect. Imagine you have an intense pain in your belly, or that you feel terrible remorse or regret for something you did, and let it "wring" your insides like a twisted piece of fabric.

After that gut-wrenching experience, Variation VII, "Ethereal," offers you the chance to experience the effort action "float," which is light, sustained and indirect. Try to make "float" as light as "wring" was heavy. Imagine that gravity has been turned off in the room, and move about with a sense of wonder and ease.

You will find that music, singing, movement, and emotion all come together in the étude "More and More," giving you a chance to stretch and strengthen your range across three differ- ent sets of qualities: heavy or light, quick or sustained, and direct or indirect. Make time during a warm-up or conditioning session to explore as many of the variations as you can. Then look for moments in the songs you are working on where you can effec- tively use those choices.

CHAPTER 17

Conclusion

Throughout this book, you've been introduced to a formidable array of powerful new ideas about singing onstage. In many ways, the first of those ideas is the most powerful. Once more, let's revisit the language I proposed to describe the job of the singing actor: "to create behavior that communicates the dramatic event." By using these words to define the work facing you, I'm inviting you to think of what you do as fundamentally creative and to think of yourself as a "create-on-demand professional."

As someone who's spent his whole life working as a "create-on-demand professional," I have a lot of firsthand experience as to what that feels like. I know how thrilling, how utterly exhilarating it can be to complete a creative project and have your work be received with enthusiasm and approval. I also know how fraught the path leading to that destination can be, the despair and frustration and uncertainty you're forced to confront when you set out to create original work, knowing that it will eventually be judged by others. When your field of endeavor is the musical stage, your performance is the creative product you will present to the world–to your teacher, your classmates, the auditors at an audition, your director, your castmates, and ultimately the audience and the critics.

In these pages, I've presented a number of tools and techniques you can use to develop the skills you need to create the best possible result you are capable of. I formulated the "SAVI" acronym and the four words it stands for–Specificity, Variety, Authenticity and Intensity–to make it easy for you to remember the key attributes of effective singing-acting, and I've described procedures that have proven effective for singing actors in pursuit of "Maximum SAVI."

But now the ball is in your court. Are you ready to "do the work"? That's the challenge you will face every day as a create-on-demand professional. Standing between you and "doing the work" is something that author Stephen Pressfield has famously described as "the Resistance." The Resistance is an insidious force of nature that seeks to distract us and prevent us from doing the work, and as a creative artist, you will do battle with it every day. The Resistance can take the form of procrastination ("I'll practice tomorrow"), perfectionism ("My work will never be good enough!"), jealousy ("It's not fair that some people get all the breaks!) or just plain fear ("I'll die of embarrassment when they see my lame-ass shit!"). As a creative warrior pursuing an artistic goal, you will find yourself engaged in a never-ending battle with The Resistance, something that Pressfield calls "The War of Art."[42]

The SAVI System was created to give you tools and techniques, procedures and ideas that will serve your pursuit of peak performance. They work when you Do The Work, but only if you Do The Work, and that means overcoming The Resistance that you understandably feel. Go back and re-read the ten axioms presented in Chapter Two. Review Chapter Five and consider what it means to train like an athlete. Ask yourself, what is standing between me and becoming the kind of singing actor I intend to be?

And then go to the practice room and Do The Work.

---

[42] For more on overcoming the Resistance, see Steven Pressfield's *The War of Art: Break Through Your Blocks* and *Win Your Inner Creative Battles* (New York: Black Irish Entertainment, 2012).

The Work Cycle of the Singing Actor

Different days bring different challenges in the life of a singing actor, and if you're savvy, you'll learn to adapt your practice habits accordingly. If you've spent any time working in the field, you've already experienced this: some days are show days, some are rehearsal days, and some days you have a class, a lesson or an audition. Some days you'll juggle several of these, and some days there'll be nothing at all on your calendar. Let's look at the role that practicing and technique play in each of these different phases of the work cycle of the singing actor.

Practicing is Not Rehearsing

When you are in a show, it probably feels like your number-one priority. We've all heard the saying, "The show must go on," which seems to suggest that everything else in our lives must take a back seat when we're in one. But what about when you're not in a show? And can you take control of your priorities even when you're in a show?

The everyday life of an artist is a mosaic of different types of activities, some of which are crucial to your professional success, while others have to do with other aspects of your life: your family, your grades, paying your bills, maintaining your health. When you are in school, you have class assignments to prepare for your voice teacher or your studio teacher, as well as other kinds of academic assignments. Juggling all these commitments is a daunting task of self-management.

In the world of elite-level performance, there is work to do every day apart from the work you do in rehearsal and preparation for a specific event. A musician works alone in the practice room every day, not just in rehearsals and concerts. Dancers take class daily as well, whether it's a ballet barre, a jazz class, or just aerobic conditioning. An athlete trains every day, regardless of whether there's a game.

It's been my experience that actors, even singing actors, are less inclined to practice daily, but incorporating daily practice into your routine can have remarkable benefits for the singing actor. You must make a concerted effort to build daily practice time into your schedule, regardless of whether you are in a show. Productivity bloggers and experts agree: "What gets scheduled gets done." Put it on your calendar and make it happen!

I recommend you build the following three ingredients into every single practice session:

1. Conditioning. Use the SAVI Workout, the SAVI Cards, and the exercises and études in this book to develop your ability to create behavior while singing, and to improve your range, agility, coordination and strength. Don't rush into working on your songs without spending some time warming up and conditioning your face, body, voice and mind. This is your time to "work on the singer"—that is, to work on *you*, rather than on any particular song.

2. Exploring. Exploration is especially important if you're preparing repertoire for class performance or rehearsal, but worth including in every practice session. Try out options and choices for a specific piece of repertoire using the SAVI Cards as a catalyst. Try leaving out the singing and use the Lip Sync exercise to explore behavioral possibilities that aren't constrained or dictated by vocal production. Visit the places you haven't yet, and consider all possibilities, even the ones that seem impossible or off the wall. Use video and your practice journal to make note of any promising discoveries.

Whether you're alone in the practice room or in the rehearsal space with your fellow ensemble members, this period of discovery is crucial to your ability to do distinctive, creative work. This is the time when you are actively exploring a piece of material to discover the full range of choices available to you and, eventually, to determine which ones will be most useful and desirable.

3. Crafting and "routining". This is probably the sort of work you associate with practicing: preparing a piece of repertoire for performance in a class, lesson or rehearsal. In this phase, you will take the rough, raw ideas that have emerged from your explorations and craft them into an organized performance. Work phrase by phrase on your material, digging deeply into the opportunities that one particular phrase offers, then repeating that process with each subsequent phrase. Link your choices together into a sequence and practice the coordinated execution of your sequence of choices. Try working under tempo or "marking," then gradually increase the intensity and speed of your execution until you reach performance conditions.

Crafting involves an element of "routining," in which "routine" is both a noun and an adjective. The noun **routine** is a "sequence of actions regularly followed," while the adjective **routine** refers to the quality attained through frequent repetition.

"Routine" may have a pejorative connotation in some situations—its synonyms include "ordinary," "standard" and "unexceptional"—but being able to create a routine in a performance is enormously valuable. When you make a sequence of choices in a performance "routine," you'll be able to execute them with a minimum of conscious attention. As you build a performance, you will arrange the choices you have arrived at for each individual phrase sequentially and master the challenge of executing them with consistency. Some refining and editing will take place during this phase of the work, as you calibrate your choices and adjust to your fellow performers, the accompaniment and the technical elements around you. Repeat your performance as often as you need to until your choices become second nature. That way, you can focus your attention elsewhere while you're performing: on your partner, the environment and the sensory input that will be the key to an effective, lifelike performance.

Crafting a Song

There's a lot a singing actor can learn about crafting a performance of a song from understanding the ways that a songwriter creates a song.

Songs are painstakingly wrought through a highly iterative process of drafting and revision. The songwriter may start out with a spark of inspiration (an image or a phrase, for example), but usually, a finished song is arrived at via an arduous process of trial and error (usually with lots and lots of both). Part of the songwriter's art is the ability to persevere with the process of writing and rewriting until, eventually, the song exists in a final form so natural and apt in its expression that it appears to have sprung fully formed from the head of the songwriter.

When it comes to books written by songwriters about their craft, Stephen Sondheim's two volumes *Finishing the Hat* and *Look, I Made A Hat* are among the best of the lot. Sondheim begins his first volume by identifying a brief set of principles that underlie everything he has written over the course of an astonishingly creative career. They are ("in no particular order," he says, "and to be written in stone"):

1. Content dictates form.
2. Less is more.
3. God is in the details.
All in the service of CLARITY,
Without which nothing else matters.[43]

These are powerful principles that offer valuable guidance not only to the writer but also to the aspiring performer of songs.

1. **"Content dictates form."** As a singing actor, you are the beneficiary of the decisions that the songwriter has already made about form. Your job is to understand that form so you can fill it and breathe life into it. Just like a sand mold in a foundry gives shape to the molten metal poured into it, a song is a vessel designed to contain and give shape to the "hot" content with which you'll infuse it.

The form of a song provides important clues about content that will guide your interpretation. You must learn to analyze that form and recognize the ways in which choices of melody, harmony, rhythm and phrase structure can express content. This is a crucial part of the "work on the song" that has been described in previous chapters.

---

[43] Stephen Sondheim, *Finishing the Hat*, (New York, Knopf, 2010), xv.

2. **"Less is more."** This phrase supposedly originated with Bauhaus architect Ludwig Mies van der Rohe, and is cited as an article of faith by art makers in all disciplines, including authors like me.

Before you embrace these words to live by, however, let's pause to consider what this advice means for the singing actor. It's common for singers to worry about "not doing enough" or "doing too much." Some singers are prone to do too much, usually out of nervousness or ego, while others, feeling fearful or distracted, find themselves paralyzed and incapable of creating the least bit of behavior.

Songs are brief, to be sure, and for that reason they rely on economy of expression for optimal impact. Despite what Sondheim's rule seems to imply, though, it does not follow that "least is most," or that doing nothing is the best choice. The successful artist creates abundantly, then selects and edits ruthlessly. In this way, you eventually find the single glance or gesture or inflection that can fully express what you wish to convey. Be prepared to throw lots of ideas away; creating in a form that values economical expression requires, as it turns out, the ability to be willfully inefficient. Chances are that you'll have to try out an endless array of ideas and choices, discarding most of them as you select and arrange the most effective ones. The path to "less" often lies through "more," if not "most."

3. **"God is in the details."** As it turns out, this is another famous dictum of Mies. What do you think it means that two of the three guiding principles of the greatest musical theater writer of the late twentieth century come from the world of architecture? This maxim suggests that artists can attain a sublime result, comparable to the perfection of our Creator's handiwork, by being scrupulously attentive to detail. The writer "sweats the details" to arrive at the perfect word, the perfect phrase, trying out many alternatives before arriving at a final choice, and the performer is well advised to follow the writer's example.

4. **"All in the service of clarity, without which nothing else matters."** I know that Sondheim sounds like a grumpy old headmaster when he makes pronouncements like this, but it's true: there's no situation in any kind of theater where the ability to create clarity isn't crucial. Even in a modern work that is totally bizarre, ambiguous, fantastical—something by Gertrude Stein, say, or Philip Glass or Richard Foreman or Robert Wilson—the individual elements and moments within that production are quite clear and specific, and the radical, aesthetic impact of the piece derives from the juxtaposition of those clearly chosen details.

It's always been my preference for singers to go easy on the "mood sauce," and instead to strive for clarity: clarity of intention, clarity of diction, clarity in choice and execution of behavior. Clarity may seem like an old-fashioned virtue, but without it, there is no drama; in the audience, the natives will grow restless because the spell of atmosphere will soon give way to boredom and confusion. For that reason, my advice to "make the action clear" is offered as the final and ultimate piece of advice for anyone who wants to "sing a song that's SAVI."

SAVI at Work in Rehearsals

All three of the activities I've just described – conditioning, exploring and crafting - should be a part of your daily practice. When you're not in a show, this routine will keep your skills sharp and your technique growing even without the daily activity of rehearsal and performance. If you use this process to prepare audition material, including sides, you'll be in top form when it's time to try out for the next gig. When you're cast in a show, your SAVI skills will serve you in every phase of the rehearsal and performance cycle.

1. Preparation. In the earliest phases of creating a performance, there is preparatory work to be done, which is the foundation on which the performance will be erected. This includes learning music and learning text. With solid music-reading skills and a good practice routine, you'll move through this phase of the work with efficiency and effectiveness so you can get to the good stuff: exploring your options, trying out behavioral choices and examining what possibilities are in the material.

2. Exploration and discovery. In the early days of the rehearsal period, the work of the singing actor is more investigative and exploratory. Your choices are provisional at first: What if the moment was like this? What if the character behaved like this? What if I tried this tempo, this gesture, this bit of blocking, this choice? Through an experimental process of trial and error, you'll work with the creative team to explore the possibilities as fully and creatively as time and circumstances permit. Of course, you'll make plenty of new choices on the spot, responding to what's happening in the moment with scene partners and other collaborators, but you must prepare outside the rehearsal room so that you are ready to make proposals, suggestions and contributions of your own. Don't underestimate the value the SAVI Cards can have as creative catalysts during this exploratory phase of the work.

Impulsive spontaneity is an especially valuable attribute to possess during the creative process of discovery, when you are exploring the full range of possibilities inherent in each moment of a performance. For this reason, it is crucial to build the skill of ouchability during your conditioning and practice sessions, so that beginning each phrase with an "ouch-y impulse" becomes second nature.

The discovery process that goes on during rehearsals is analytical as well as intuitive and organic. It's crucial to determine where the dings are and which ones are most important as you consider the changes and adjustments that will be useful for communicating the dramatic event. You will find yourself asking, Does it help to have a ding here? Is making a change more effective than not making one? Am I getting anything from my partner in the present moment that would prompt an adjustment? Is the environment affecting me?

When dances are being created, it may feel like the choreographer and her assistants are the boss and you're merely there to execute their ideas. Good choreographers prepare extensively before rehearsal so that the chaotic, complex work of "setting" the choreography can be done efficiently. The process of creating a dance, however, is more collaborative than you might initially assume. Being a dancer working with a choreographer has the potential to be very rewarding creatively. Once the choreographer sees you execute a move or phrase, their opinion about the effectiveness of a movement is likely to change, and there can be a great deal of give-and-take between the choreographer, dancers and music team as the choreography evolves over the course of rehearsals. Don't be surprised if you're invited to contribute a movement or an idea, or to adapt a movement according to the unique properties of your body.

During this exploratory phase, the work that was once in flux eventually becomes "set," and the creative team makes a transition from discovery to crafting.

3. Crafting your performance score. Later in the rehearsal process, once you've done your exploration (or the bulk of it, at least), you'll work on crafting a performance that will incorporate your discoveries into a coherent, consistent sequence of behaviors. This must be coordinated with the temporal flow of the musical score, the work of the ensemble and the technical aspects of the production.

In these latter phases of the work, discovering new ideas through impulsive choice-making becomes less important. Now it's time to select the choices that work best—on your own and in collaboration with the director, your fellow actors and the other members of your production team—and learn to execute them consistently.

In the middle of a rehearsal period, you will be in the process of deciding what specific choices will be a part of the performance score. Each moment and sequence of moments is examined by the creative team using a collaborative process. Sometimes this work is done in a start-and-stop manner, with choices reconsidered and edited on the spot. Sometimes the work is done via notes given at the end of a run through of a scene or section, or a run through of the full work: the director wants to go back and reconsider one or more choices that are part of the sequence.

As the ensemble works together to build a performance, even if it's just you and your accompanist building a performance to present in class, everyone needs to know what to expect from their fellow ensemble members so that the group's efforts can be effectively coordinated. Once you've arrived at a choice for a moment in a song, you'll be expected to re-create that choice reliably and consistently, without sacrificing its freshness or the illusion of spontaneity. This is especially true in performance, and a long run will challenge you to find ways to "get ouchable" and remain fresh and impulsive even as you execute the same sequence of music, words, and behavioral choices show after show.

4. In the late stages of rehearsal. During the final run-throughs, technical rehearsals, dress rehearsals and previews of a show, your "behavior score" is still being finalized. You've made most of your choices and arranged them in a coordinated sequence so that they're ready to be executed in real time. Some choices are challenging and tricky and will require special attention when those moments arise. Effort and energy must be managed, as the performer discovers where they can coast or ease up a bit and when they must turn up the intensity. This raises issues of stamina and focus. The executive function of the performer is called into play.

During this time, you will get notes and changes from the director, the choreographer, the conductor, and, if you're working on a new show, the writers. This will mean you have to modify certain aspects of your performance while retaining others. During this phase of the work, you will find it especially useful to have a notebook handy in which to take down notes and review the changes as part of your mental preparation for the performance. Your skills of sequencing and self-management will be tested to the limit during this period.

In addition, you will find yourself performing with ever-increasing levels of intensity as you move toward performance. You are more and more secure with the material you've learned and memorized, and thus able to tackle each moment with confidence and energy and without the constraints of fear or vagueness. I encourage my students to adopt this part of the "performance mindset" as early in the process as possible. You need to fully investigate the range of energy and intensity you can bring to your moments onstage, and to become familiar with what it is like to work in a fully energized state. The choices that you make will be different when you are fully committed, fully energized, and ready to bring more voice, more behavior and more life to every moment.

Every performer learns when it is useful to go "full out" and when it may be advisable to "mark" their moments in rehearsal. When you are "marking" your performance, you need to "hit the marks" expected of you—accurate blocking, timing, choreography, etc.—while conserving your energy so as not to wear yourself out or risk injury. This will be especially useful during technical rehearsals, when you may be called upon to do a short section of the show over and over while lighting, scenery, sound, projections and other aspects of the technical production are coordinated. Use this time to focus on the phrases in the section being rehearsed and bring the greatest possible level of specificity and clarity to your behavior each time.

In the creation of a show, these tasks usually occur in chronological order, but especially in the creation of a new show, the nature of the work can change suddenly and unexpectedly. A scene gets rewritten, a song gets replaced, a character gets rethought, and suddenly the performer moves from polishing to exploring and crafting once again.

5. In performance. The most demanding of the five phases, performance calls upon you to execute a planned sequence of choices in a way that seems spontaneous, with what Stanislavski called "the illusion of the first time." Performance involves considerable pressure and stress, the extremes of emotional, vocal and physical expression, and the difficult task of "hitting every mark" in a demanding score and sequence of choices, often for periods of an hour or more without any chance to rest or recover.

As you do this, you must account for the appearance of spontaneity that all good performances require. In fact, knowing how and when to get ouchable is a key to creating the "illusion of the first time." Nothing does more to diminish the quality of spontaneity and authenticity in a performance than a lack of ouchability. Ouchability is the magic ingredient that lifts behavior out of the mechanical and makes it seem fresh and immediate.

When you're in a show, everything in your day is organized toward delivering the best show possible. That show is a fully planned event in which every aspect of the show is "set," the choices fixed and frozen. Your task is to execute the choices that were devised in rehearsal in a manner that is persuasive and lifelike, fully energized and fully committed. This becomes an interesting challenge for shows that run over an extended period of time. After a few performances (or a few weeks), the choices become well learned and "routine," yet they must never appear routine or rote to the spectator.

Even when you're in a performance that's "set," there are unpredictable elements in play: your health, your fellow performers, the presence of replacements or understudies. And as lyricist Oscar Hammerstein reminds us, the audience in the theater is a "big black giant" which adds a different energy to every performance.

The best professionals know they must resist the temptation to go through the motions of a performance. A thorough warm-up before a show will ensure your face, voice, body and mind are optimally poised to execute the tasks ahead, and if you awaken your senses, you'll be ready to respond to the opportunities that make this performance unique.

There will always be mistakes, but every mistake is an opportunity to bring the performance to life, to bring it into the "now." The smallest mistake or departure from the routine has the potential to rouse you into a more alert, active state of mind if you approach it with the right spirit.

Finale Ultimo: The SAVI Anthem

To help you remember the fundamental SAVI principles, I set them to music in "A Song That's SAVI," a little ditty whose semi-ironic subtitle is "The SAVI Anthem." For a truly soul-stirring experience, gather around the piano for a sing-along, using the sheet music in the back of the book. If that's not possible, then go to the Book Extras section on the website[44] to hear the song, and read the lyrics below as you listen.

> Verse 1.
>
> When I sing, I will create behavior
> That communicates the dramatic event phrase
> by phrase.
> Each time I raise my voice in song,
> I'll make a specific choice in song,
> And I'll sing A Song That's SAVI all of my days.
>
> Verse 2.
>
> When I sing, I will create behavior
> That communicates the dramatic event phrase
> by phrase.
> I'll sing with authenticity,
> I'll always express myself truthfully,
> And I'll sing A Song That's SAVI all of my days.

---

[44] www.savisingingactor.com/book-extras

Verse 3.

When I sing, I will create behavior
That communicates the dramatic event phrase
by phrase.
As I begin to sing each phrase,
Variety comes when I "ding" each phrase
And I'll sing A Song That's SAVI all of my days.

Verse 4.

When I sing, I will create behavior
That communicates the dramatic event phrase
by phrase.
My work will have intensity,
And, when it is called for, immensity,
And I'll sing A Song That's SAVI all of my days.

Verse 5.

When I sing, I will create behavior
That communicates the dramatic event phrase
by phrase.
I won't play mood or atmosphere
I'll strive to make my actions clear,
And I'll sing A Song That's SAVI all of my days.

Within you is the capacity to create great work on the musical stage. It's an iterative process, a matter of trial and error, one that requires passion, patience, persistence, playfulness and an unrelenting sense of purpose. Here in my hometown, fans of the Philadelphia 76ers say, "Trust the process." You may not be experiencing the success you seek yet, but if you're patient and do the work, great things surely await you.

Teachers, Check out the MTEA!

I helped found the Musical Theater Educators Alliance International (www.musicaltheatereducators.org) 20 years ago, and it presently includes hundreds of members representing schools all over the world. Their membership is a who's who of generous, talented teachers and artists working in the field of musical theater. They publish a journal and hold annual conferences. If you're serious about teaching musical theater (or aspire to do so one day), you need to be part of this organization.

Sheet Music

Sheet music for many of the exercises described in this book can be found on the following pages. Downloadable PDFs of the music and karaoke-style "SAVI Tracks" for many of these songs can be found at www.savisingingactor.com/book-extras.

Here I Am

Charles Gilbert

Slowly, with feeling ♩= 60

Come To Me/Get Away From Me
Two SAVI Etudes

Charles Gilbert

I Have A New Idea

SAVI Etude

Charles Gilbert

Ding and Sing

SAVI Etude

Charles Gilbert

A Five Note Phrase

SAVI Étude

Charles Gilbert

Sing a five note phrase
As the mu-sic plays.
How it will a-maze
Sung in dif-f'rent ways.
Mo-di-fy your gaze.
That will earn you praise.
Prac-tice al-ways pays
With this five note phrase.

up a half step
with each repeat

A Five Note Phrase (Canon version)

SAVI Étude

Charles Gilbert

Moderato ♩ = 100

up a half step
with each repeat

A Five Note Phrase (Mirror Canon)

SAVI Étude

Charles Gilbert

ABC Song (for One-Two Focus Shifts)

SAVI Etude

Aught of Art

SAVI Étude

Charles Gilbert

Who would know aught of art must learn, act and then take his ease.

Who would know aught of art must learn, act and then take his ease.

More and More (Laban Variations)

SAVI Étude

Charles Gilbert

Var. II: Lightly (DAB)

More and more and   more and more and   more and more and   more and more!

More and more and   more and more and   more and more and   more and more!   up a half step with each repeat

Var. III: Valse (GLIDE)

More   and   more   and   more   and   more   and   more   and

more   and   more   and   more!   More   and   more   and   more   and

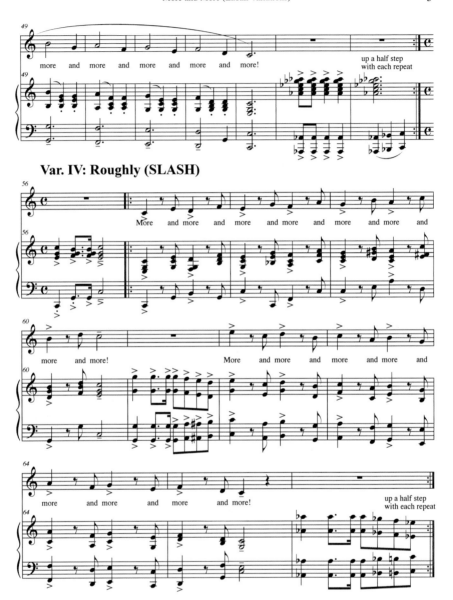

more and more and more and more and more!

up a half step
with each repeat

Var. IV: Roughly (SLASH)

More and more and more and more and more and

more and more! More and more and more and more and

more and more and more and more!

up a half step
with each repeat

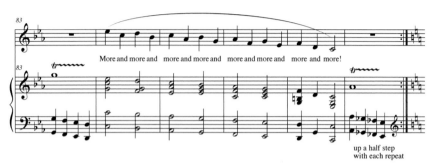

More and more and more and more and more and more and more and more!

up a half step
with each repeat

Var. VI: Ethereal (FLOAT)

More and more and more and more and more and more and more and more!

mp

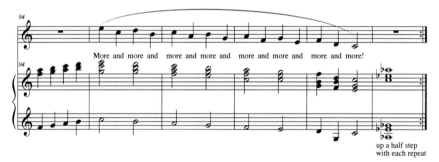

More and more and more and more and more and more and more and more!

up a half step
with each repeat

A Song That's SAVI

The SAVI Anthem

Charles Gilbert

1. When I sing, I will create behavior
That communicates the dramatic event
Phrase by phrase.
Each time I raise my voice in song,
I'll make a specific choice in song,
And I'll sing a song that's SAVI
All of my days.

2. I'll sing with authenticity,
I'll always express myself truthfully.

3. As I begin to sing each phrase
Variety comes when I "ding" each phrase.

4. My work will have intensity
And, when it is called for, immensity.

5. I won't play mood or atmosphere.
I'll strive to make my actions clear.

I'll Be Known

from "Leading Lady"

Charles Gilbert

I'll Be Known

I'll Be Known

I'll Be Known

blend in - to the sce - ne - ry, I'll have a life that I can call my own! Per -

haps I won't be fa - mous, but dam - mit, I'll be known!

CURTAIN CALL

First of all, thank you, gentle reader, for your interest and atten-tion. This book was born out of the desire to create something useful, and my dearest wish is that you will find it so. If you want to share any thoughts about what you've read with me, I am eager to hear from you. And if you want to share your thoughts with prospective future readers as well, please take a minute to leave an online review. Links to the places you can do that and to other book extras can be found at savisingingactor.com/book-extras.

Thanks to the hundreds of students who came along for the ride as I strove to shape an inchoate mass of ideas and aspira-tions about musical theater performance into a coherent peda-gogy. Thanks to the teachers who first encouraged my interests in music and theater: Margaret McCann, Florence Girlamo, Patrick McDade, Robert Stuart, Larry Wilker, Dorothy Louise, Larry Carra, Leon Katz and many others. Thanks to my classmates and friends at Carnegie Mellon University and Theater Express, who sup-ported me as I took the next steps down the path that would be my life's journey: John Mangano, Jan Kirschner, Jed Harris, Caren Harder and especially Bill Turner, who not only said "yes" when I proposed writing a musical about presidential assassins but also hired the woman who would eventually become my wife to sing the lead in an opera of his that I was music-directing. Thanks to the teachers who helped me recognize my potential as an educator: Tom Watson, Peter Vagenas, Richard Brown, and the other teach-ers who were my first colleagues at the University of Delaware; you were kind and gracious in your mentorship at a time when I'm sure I was an insufferable young Turk. Thanks to the visionaries at the University of the Arts who thought I'd be the right person to help them start a musical theater program, most especially Evan Solot and Stephen Jay but also my many colleagues in the Ira Brind School of Theater Arts. I bow reverently to the late H. Wesley Balk, the teacher and author whose work was a seminal influence on me. Thanks to the members of the Musical Theater Educators Alliance, a remarkably supportive and generous crew, especially Joe Deer, Cary Libkin, Meg Bussert, Jonathan Flom, Lara Teeter, Tom Albert, Kim Moke and Søren Møller; your friendship and collegiality mean the world to me.

During the creation of this book, I was blessed to have the support of a phenomenal crew. A round of applause, please, for my early readers, including the "SAVI Book Club" (especially Richard Cerato, Matthew Hultgren and Mitchell Hansen) and the "SAVI Soldiers" of THEA 475, whose feedback was enormously helpful. Mary Ellen Grant Kennedy, a beloved colleague, provided invaluable feedback as well as decades of friendship. Editors Chantel Hamilton and Jessica Hatch helped me wrangle the manuscript into shape, and Jody Johnson provided business coaching when it became clear that SAVI was more than just a book. Sarah Romig at P'unk Avenue made a brilliant contribution by designing the SAVI logo, the cover of the book and the SAVI Cards, while Chris Loupos brought his unique photographic talents to the SAVI picture cards that appear as spot illustrations in the book. Aaron Bell, Jaz Blain, Angelina Capone, Yui Matsuzaki, Krystal Ortega and Jelani Stuart are the six shining faces on the SAVI picture cards. Stalwart assistant Madison Claus proves herself ever more invaluable with each passing week, earning my heartfelt gratitude.

And finally, endless thanks and love to my amazing wife and partner, D'Arcy Webb, the Speech Diva, a talented educator and performer in her own right but also the most supportive spouse I could ever hope to have. How lucky I am to be worthy of your love!